ADVENTURES IN COMMUNITY SCIENCE

Library of Congress Control Number: 2022944300

Designed by Lisa Smith and Jack Chappell
Cover design by Lisa Smith
Illustrations by Lily Smith
All photos by the author unless otherwise noted
Type set in Frutiger/Yonder/True North

ISBN: 978-0-7643-6575-1
Printed in China

Published by Schiffer Kids
An imprint of Schiffer Publishing, Ltd.
4880 Lower Valley Road
Atglen, PA 19310
Phone: (610) 593-1777; Fax: (610) 593-2002
Email: info@schifferbooks.com
Web: www.schiffer-kids.com

For our complete selection of fine books on this and related subjects, please visit our website at www.schifferbooks.com. You may also write for a free catalog.

Schiffer Publishing's titles are available at special discounts for bulk purchases for sales promotions or premiums. Special editions, including personalized covers, corporate imprints, and excerpts, can be created in large quantities for special needs. For more information, contact the publisher.

ADVENTURES IN COMMUNITY SCIENCE

— RON SMITH —

ILLUSTRATIONS BY LILY SMITH

NOTES FROM THE FIELD AND A
— HOW-TO GUIDE FOR SAVING SPECIES AND —
PROTECTING BIODIVERSITY

Schiffer **Kids**®

4880 Lower Valley Road, Atglen, PA 19310

DEDICATION/ACKNOWLEDGMENTS

I wish to acknowledge the thousands of students who have explored the natural world with me over the past three decades. It is their curiosity and enthusiasm that fuels my own. To my friends and colleagues of the Haddonfield School District, the Academy of Natural Sciences of Drexel University, National Audubon Hog Island Family Camp, and Pinelands Preservation Alliance, who have endorsed and embraced the projects and studies I have conducted over the years, thank you all.

To my mentors, Craig Newberger and Trudy Phillips, who not only gave me my first opportunity to teach in the outdoors but have also inspired educators and students alike for nearly five decades, this book would not have been possible without my first steps with you on a mossy island path.

To Russell Juelg, Carleton Montgomery, Dr. James Spotila, Dr. Amanda Dey, Dr. Larry Niles, Dr. Nellie Tsipoura, Dr. Dane Ward, Roger Thomas, Dr. David Velinsky, and Dr. John Dighton, who helped me establish the foundations of science in my work. Thanks to Karen Acton for her creative input and support on this project and to Stephanie Middleton for her review efforts for the book. Special thanks to Scott Weidensaul for reviewing the entire text and for inspiring my nature writing and community science projects.

To my editor, Tracee Groff, whose enthusiastic vision for this book inspired my writing and future projects. Many thanks to Ann Charles for her contributions and careful review of the text and every detail of the many photos, activities, and graphs.

To my parents, who gave me a childhood of exploration and wonder. To my entire family, with whom I have shared many adventures. To my brother, Michael, who was my first partner in nature studies. I love you all.

To my children. Gabriel, thank you for being my partner as we protect and study nature and for joining me on every community science adventure. Lily, thank you for your creative partnership and vision on this project. Your illustrations and photographs make the stories come alive.

To my wife, Lisa. No one could be more supportive, creative, patient, and enthusiastic about my adventures than you. This book is dedicated to you and our family.

CONTENTS

You are capable of more than you know. Choose a goal that seems right for you, and strive to be the best, however hard the path. Aim high, behave honorably. Prepare to be alone at times and to endure failure. Persist! The world needs all you can give.

–E. O. WILSON

★ 🌲 ★

FOREWORD

BY DR. JAMES SPOTILA

CONSERVATION BIOLOGIST, BETZ CHAIR PROFESSOR OF ENVIRONMENTAL SCIENCE (EMERITUS), FORMER DIRECTOR OF THE CENTER FOR BIODIVERSITY AND CONSERVATION AT DREXEL UNIVERSITY, AND AUTHOR OF *SAVING SEA TURTLES*

We can all participate in "Adventures in Community Science." In this book, Ron Smith provides a compelling argument for conservation in our own backyards and shows you how to do it. Community scientists study and document nature in their local neighborhoods, parks, and natural areas. From horseshoe crabs on the bay, to shorebirds on the beach, to insects in the garden, this book brings the reader into the adventure and demonstrates how they can become community scientists. Ron offers hands-on, explorative, inquiry-based investigations that allow students to do science instead of merely reading about science. Within the chapters, students will practice science in a way that develops skills, establishes partnerships and collaboration, and addresses meaningful questions with emphasis on place-based study. Curiosity, creativity, and communication are the keys to developing a scientific mind.

Society needs people who think critically, examine data, ask questions, and are dedicated to making a difference. Whether a student will become a teacher, lawyer, plumber, scientist, or podcast expert, that student will need to be able to make observations, think logically, and ask good questions. Young people develop these abilities by learning to think critically, to investigate, and to engage science. This book is an adventure-based, how-to guide for practicing meaningful science in our backyards and communities. Students will become community scientists who make the planet more sustainable for all species, including our own. Finally, not only is this book a blueprint for doing community-based science, it is a call to young people to connect to the natural world and make a difference.

INTRODUCTION

ALL HANDS ON DECK!

Species all over the planet are in trouble. Habitat loss, invasive species, and pollution have impacted creatures from large mammals to tiny insects. There are dedicated scientists and conservation organizations that lead the charge to protect species and work to ensure the recovery of their populations. As the threats have increased over the past couple of decades and the list of species in trouble grows, it has become necessary to rally more people to the cause of biodiversity study and protection. These volunteers are known as community scientists and are people just like you and me who have an interest in nature, science, and the health of the environment.

With training and some time dedicated to any number of projects, you too can become a partner in the conservation movement. Along the way you will assist scientists; help guide conservation in the direction of saving species; learn more about nature and science; share the experiences with friends, family, and community; and celebrate the joy of helping our fellow species on planet Earth.

This book provides a window into the adventures of some young community scientists who, like you, care about nature and choose to make a difference.

PART ONE

THE MAKING OF A
COMMUNITY SCIENTIST

CHAPTER 1

EARLY DAYS OF A YOUNG NATURALIST

We drove down the long, straight stretch of road on a warm spring afternoon. Up ahead, a small mound was slowly making its way across the street. We slowed down, and my dad put on the blinkers. I hopped out of the car and approached the small turtle. As I did, another car approached from the opposite direction, also slowing down as it came near. A little girl smiled from the back seat as I held up the reptile to show them the reason for our stop. Walking a few feet into the woods in the direction the turtle was traveling, I carefully placed the box turtle on the ground, and almost immediately he popped his head out from the front hinge of his shell and moved, as fast as a box turtle can go, into the shrubs.

I grew up about 20 miles east of Philadelphia on the edge of a vast wilderness. The New Jersey Pine Barrens is found right in the middle of one of the most populated regions in the United States. With about a million acres of forest, swamp, and lakes, it is the largest coastal wilderness between Boston and Washington, DC. My family moved here in 1975, around the same time that much of this forest was protected by the State of New Jersey. Like most kids, the adventures of my youth took place in the open space and natural areas that were available. At the time, I did not know how fortunate I was to be able to explore this special ecosystem. During my early years, the region would be celebrated around the world as a biosphere reserve and, here in the United States, as the nation's first national reserve. To me it was my backyard.

On any given day I could choose to explore a number of narrow, sandy paths that extended out into the forest. In those hours, days, months, and years, I would learn so much about nature, and, on occasion, I would come to realize that not only could I learn from my walks through the woods and paddles on the lakes, but I could help protect the creatures that brought me such joy.

Every spring and early summer, box turtles would venture out in search of food and mates and nesting sites. Though there was good habitat available, many turtles would still end up crossing roads. It was always a very sad occasion when I would come across an individual that did not make it to the other side. So, every time we

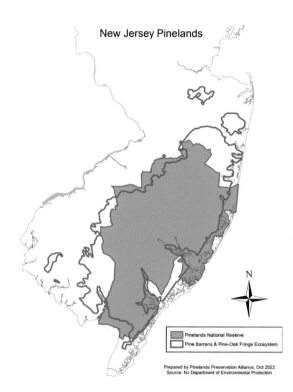

New Jersey Pinelands

Pinelands National Reserve
Pine Barrens & Pine-Oak Fringe Ecosystem

Prepared by Pinelands Preservation Alliance, Oct 2022
Source: NJ Department of Environmental Protection

would drive off to the store or baseball practice, my eyes were set to the road. It became a family project, and though back then I was not keeping track of the numbers, I am certain that hundreds of box turtles found their way safely as a result of the assistance we offered whenever we pulled over for a rescue. I took such great joy in saving a turtle and loved to share our family rescue stories with my cousins and friends. **Soon this became a community effort, and we would compare notes on how many, male or female, and where the latest rescue took place.** So it went for years to come, and I still look out for box turtles when I journey to the Pine Barrens or other natural places.

An eastern box turtle crosses a road.

It did not occur to me when I was young that my future was being forged by simple observations and activities in nature. I consider myself very fortunate that my only limitations during these early explorations were how far my legs could carry me and the promises made to my family about being safe while outside. Though my explorations took me miles down wooded trails and included overnight stays on a small island in the lake near my home and navigating around swampy thickets with briar, it was often right in my backyard that quiet observations would lead me to the realization that so many species need our help and that **I could make a difference.**

Every spring, life would emerge from curious places. All around our house the window wells along the base of the foundation allowed light into the basement. The lights from my home attracted insects, and, in turn, the insects attracted toads. Once the toads made the leap down into the leaf litter at the bottom of the well, the smooth aluminum sides would not allow for their escape. Not only did we regularly survey the half-dozen wells for trapped toads, which would then be lifted to freedom, but we promoted this activity to friends and family who also had window wells around their homes—again, an early attempt to organize our community rescue efforts.

It was a conservation issue near home during my college years that would help solidify my lifetime dedication to the natural world. As boys, my brother and I were proud of our accumulated list of species about which we had gathered countless observations. No species could match snakes for their impressive presence and, in terms of our skills as naturalists, testing of our field mettle. We were always respectful and cautious around snakes. The only venomous species in southern New Jersey was the timber rattlesnake (listed as an endangered species in New Jersey in 1979). Only a couple of miles from our home was a hibernaculum (hibernation den) for this species.

▲ A window well is an unintended trap for toads and other creatures.

◄ A young Fowler's toad rescued from a window well

DID YOU KNOW ?

Timber rattlesnakes may hibernate with snakes of other species.

Long was the list of friends with whom my brother and I shared our observations of this amazing species. When I was away for college in New England, a housing development project was approved in the Pine Barrens close to my family's home. I did not know about the project until reports of an endangered species controversy came to light. The developer had hired a survey company to conduct an inventory of endangered species on hundreds of acres of forest and swamp. No endangered species were found. Development began, and then timber rattlesnakes began showing up on streets, in gardens, and on driveways. After several years of efforts to protect the snakes, while also allowing for development, the rattlesnake population disappeared. Had my brother and I been asked if there were snakes on the property, we could have easily brought anyone to see them.

Rattlesnake habitat in the Pine Barrens

Today every conservation organization around the planet has sounded the alarm. Many species are facing extinction! It will take more than laws, governments, and the handful of dedicated scientists on the front lines of conservation to bring these species back from the edge. I have made a promise to myself and the planet that every day I will dedicate myself to studying, sharing, and protecting the amazing biodiversity all around us.

— CHAPTER 2 —

THE NEED FOR COMMUNITY SCIENCE

BIODIVERSITY IN TROUBLE

The species and projects described in this book are not what most people think of when they hear about species in trouble. Large, exotic mammals on exhibit in zoos and wildlife parks capture our attention. Giant pandas are hanging on in forest patches that are but a small fragment of what used to be found across much of China. Elephants have been killed in large numbers for their tusks in Africa. Many of our great whale species are struggling to recover after centuries of being hunted in every ocean. These are the familiar faces of the world's biodiversity crisis.

But what about the less familiar faces? Look closely into the eyes of a horseshoe crab. It may be difficult for many to love a species that lives on the ocean bottom, looks part scorpion and part crab, and emerges only for a few weeks under the cover of darkness on forgotten beaches. The secret life of tree frogs does indeed keep them safe, but it also keeps them out of view from most people who might come to know that many are in trouble. A flock of shorebirds dropping in on a beach is an amazing sight. Though a couple of hundred individuals might seem like a lot of birds, these flocks used to be 10 times their current population. Lightning bugs entertain us on warm summer evenings, but their flashes are more interesting to many than the insects that make them. **All of these species need our help too!**

DID YOU KNOW ?

More than 25% of mammal species and 50% of amphibians across the planet are in danger of going extinct.

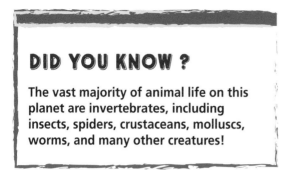
Toads, turtles, and timber rattlesnakes—it seems that many of the creatures I studied and observed in my youth are now less abundant than they once were. I frequently visit the house and property where I grew up. The changes that have occurred on the landscape and the impact of people are evident. Many of the sand roads I ventured down as a child are now wide and paved. The woodlands have been carved up into properties where houses now sit. The huckleberry and sedges that dominate the understory of a natural pine forest have often been converted to manicured lawns that require fertilizers and pesticides to maintain. Traffic, noise, and pollution have increased while natural habitat and diversity have declined.

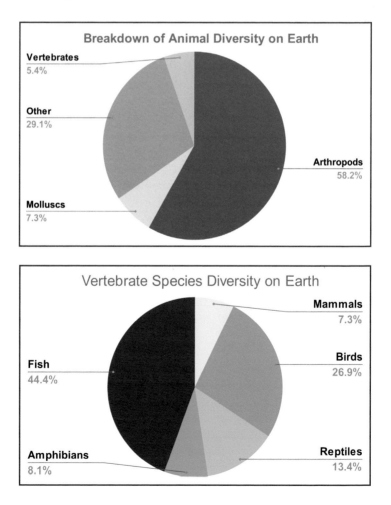

Breakdown of Animal Diversity on Earth

Vertebrates 5.4%

Other 29.1%

Molluscs 7.3%

Arthropods 58.2%

Vertebrate Species Diversity on Earth

Mammals 7.3%

Birds 26.9%

Fish 44.4%

Reptiles 13.4%

Amphibians 8.1%

The box turtles I helped across roads as a child have been collected in large numbers and sold as pets. Freshwater mussels in the streams and rivers have been pushed aside by invasive clams. In the backyards of my neighborhood, pollution has reduced the incidence of lightning bugs. Tree frogs in the Pine Barrens have less habitat than they once did. Shorebirds have less space to feed and roost, while horseshoe crabs have less beach to spawn due to climate change. The threats to wildlife in our backyards and around the world come in many forms, and we must face them all and take action.

Should we care about biodiversity? Have we been called to be stewards of life on Earth? Simply stated, yes! Is it true that every species is needed in the ecosystems of our planet? Yes! Is our well-being and health tied to the diversity of life on this planet? Absolutely! Perhaps it is this fact that is the key to getting conservation work done. Our lives are connected to the lives of every species on the planet. Their Earth is our Earth.

Today the practice and sharing of science is so very important to the way we view the world around us. We must be active participants in science, and we must share good science with others. There are so many opportunities to do so. In the pages that follow, you will read about young people and their efforts to save species and make a difference. People just like you are inspired to get up a bit earlier, roll up their sleeves, put on some gloves, and be on the front lines of a movement that will transform how science and nature are valued, used, and applied in our world. It is time, and you are needed. **Join us for adventures in community science!**

The entire Community Science Kids Team gathers for a photo in front of a pollinator garden they helped plant.

PART TWO

ADVENTURES IN
COMMUNITY SCIENCE

CHAPTER 3

HORSESHOE CRAB RESCUE

INVITATION TO ADVENTURE

Travel to the Atlantic coast, where the world's largest gathering of horseshoe crabs come to spawn. Millions of horseshoe crabs emerge on the evening tides of May and June to lay their eggs. Millions of crabs equals billions of eggs, but these ancient creatures need your help. Some are flipped over by waves, and many get trapped by pilings, seawalls, concrete, and other human structures. Without the rescue effort, many would perish and the population would dwindle. **We need your help to save this unique species, one that is older than the dinosaurs!**

Horseshoe crab heroes needed!
Horseshoe crabs trapped along
the Delaware Bay coast.

Not actually crabs at all, horseshoe crabs are more closely related to spiders and scorpions than crustaceans. Named for the shape of their shell, or carapace, these marine invertebrates migrate into the bays of the East Coast of the United States seeking quiet, sandy beaches to spawn (lay and fertilize their eggs). With a tough exoskeleton and six pairs of legs to feed and crawl, horseshoe crabs leave the water only to lay their eggs in the spring and early summer.

The female digs down into the sand and deposits eggs, which will be fertilized by the males—often attached to the back of the female. The tiny green eggs, which carpet the bay beaches, are food for many creatures, including shorebirds, which have flown thousands of miles for the feast, and many other aquatic species that live in the coastal waters. The eggs that survive will develop and, after a few weeks, young horseshoe crabs emerge. In order to grow, they must shed their hard exoskeleton. Before they reach adult size, they may do this up to 20 times! When the crabs are young, they stay in the protected waters near the shore.

In about eight years or so, they will be adults, ready to return to the beaches to spawn as their parents did before them. A female will emerge on the evening high tides to lay her eggs. Males, with specially shaped front legs, will attach to the shell of a female.

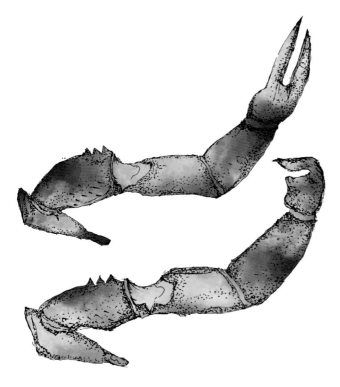

Difference between a female front leg (*above*) and a male front leg (*below*)

Other males may wait nearby, hoping to fertilize some of her eggs. The cycle of life begins again. The adult crabs will migrate out of the bay in late summer and spend the winter in deeper water offshore.

For over 100 years, horseshoe crabs have faced danger from humans. Formerly collected for fertilizer, they are now harvested for bait. Some are taken to labs where their blood is collected, because it is used to check medicines for contamination by bacteria. Rising seas are eroding beaches where crabs spawn, and on other beaches, human structures such as seawalls and pilings trap them. The efforts of volunteers save tens of thousands of crabs every spring. Horseshoe crabs have been around much longer than dinosaurs, but now they are threatened with extinction. All four species of horseshoe crabs around the world face troubles due to human activity. **At the same time, it is people who can save them!**

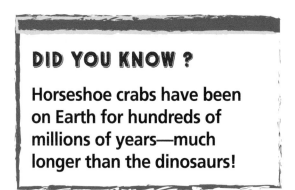

DID YOU KNOW ?

Horseshoe crabs have been on Earth for hundreds of millions of years—much longer than the dinosaurs!

Two smaller male horseshoe crabs attempt to latch on the back of the larger female as she searches for a spot to deposit her eggs.

HORSESHOE CRAB RESCUE

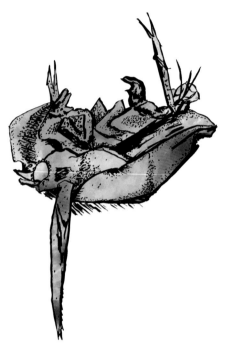

We turned onto New Jersey Avenue, and we could smell the bay. That earthy, warm smell of mud, marsh, and salty water let us know we had arrived. It was 4 a.m. and still dark, so we could not see the water. Parking at the seawall by what is known as Fishing Beach, we scrambled for our first look. It was late May and a new moon, so we were planning for a big rescue. Still sleepy, we put on our headlamps and jackets. The breeze, though chilly, was welcome because it would keep the bugs down during the day ahead.

As we looked down from the seawall, our lights revealed an alien world. We had to plan our drop onto the sand carefully because there were horseshoe crabs everywhere! The rounded backs of some were plowing through the sand on a return trip to the bay. Other crabs were overturned. Trying to use their long, pointy tails to turn over, their legs wriggled frantically.

Horseshoe crabs overturned after high tide recedes

Horseshoe crabs stranded!
Horseshoe crabs caught in rubble after a storm.

We looked over to Sasha, and she nodded that she was ready. Notebook and pencil in hand, she would have the job of documenting every crab rescued. Sasha would note the location, male or female, and whether the crab rescue was a flip or a trap. Flipped crabs merely had to be turned over so they could return to the bay, but trapped crabs had to be dug out, lifted free, or untangled from whatever kept them from escaping. With a couple of new rescuers along for the day, we reviewed the identification of male and female crabs. Larger crabs were usually female, and the males have a front leg that is shaped so he can latch on to a female. Only crabs flipped or trapped were to be handled, and we reminded the group not to put their hands in the joint between the head and abdomen, since pinched fingers would result. Crabs were never to be picked up by their tails, as this could injure the animals.

In a tight line, we marched down the beach at low tide, calling out—flip male, trap female . . .

The pages of the field notebook filled quickly at this, our first beach. Shovels were used to dig out crabs under slabs of concrete, and we used our phones to take pictures of crabs that had tag numbers from an ongoing state and federal study. An hour later we finished site 1. With four to go, we scrambled back to the car. **This day we would rescue over 3,000 crabs from five beaches.** The last rescues of the day came as the now-rising tide crept toward us. Exhausted after almost six hours of rescue, we celebrated the day with an early lunch and a pledge that we would return next week to do it all over again!

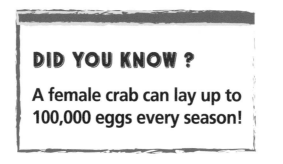

DID YOU KNOW ?

A female crab can lay up to 100,000 eggs every season!

TRAPPED & FLIPPED CRABS
AT FIVE BEACHES ON THE DELAWARE BAY

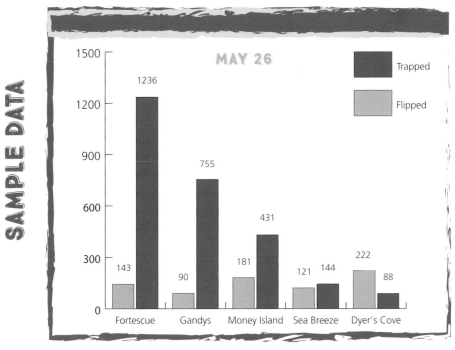

MAY 26

SAMPLE DATA

Trapped
Flipped

Fortescue: 143, 1236
Gandys: 90, 755
Money Island: 181, 431
Sea Breeze: 121, 144
Dyer's Cove: 222, 88

DATA SET FROM ONE OF OUR RESCUES

FIND OUT...

- How many total crabs were rescued on this day?
- What beach do you think had the most human habitat disturbance? How do you know?
- What information should you gather from every site, other than the number of crabs rescued?

Our rescue brought us to the Delaware Bay, but you can count and rescue horseshoe crabs along the entire Eastern Seaboard from Maine to the Gulf of Mexico. Find out from local conservation groups, or your state wildlife agencies, where crabs are known to gather. Research your site and the horseshoe crab activity in your region. Crab counts are conducted on the high tides as they spawn, but rescues are best done on the low tides, where trapped crabs are most accessible. Be sure to check local regulations or laws that may limit access to spawning beaches. Join an existing effort if such a project exists. If not, work with your family or through your school, scout groups, or naturalist clubs to initiate a count or rescue. **We helped initiate the rescues in our region, and you can do the same!**

Be careful not to disturb other species such as shorebirds, which may be feeding on horseshoe crab eggs or be present on the beach during your study. If you are going out at night, bring a flashlight or headlamp and always go in teams. The beach can have biting insects, so be prepared. Long-sleeve shirts, hats, and bandannas can help keep bugs off during the rescue and can also help protect you from the sun. If there is a lot of debris on the beach, long pants and closed-toe shoes will keep your feet and legs protected. A water bottle and snacks will be needed too! A small hand shovel is useful in case you have to dig a crab out from under some structure. Remember, rescue only crabs in trouble. Do not dig up crabs that may be spawning.

Keep careful notes and take pictures to document your efforts and the issues that horseshoe crabs face at your study site. We recommend a journal where you can keep notes from multiple visits. Rite in the Rain (www.riteintherain.com) notebooks are sturdy and water resistant. **Share your data with your team, your school, and local conservation groups.**

DID YOU KNOW ?

Some shorebirds fly for up to five days from South America to feed on horseshoe crab eggs!

Horseshoe crabs spawning amid shorebirds. Crab eggs are an important food source for the shorebirds. *Photo credit: Alexandra McDonnell*

CHECKLIST FOR YOUR ADVENTURE

- **Long Pants**
- **Old Sneakers**
- **Headlamp**
- **Shovel**
- **Pencil**

- **Notebook**
- **Jacket**
- **Phone/Camera**
- **Water Bottle**

Online Resources

Horseshoe Crab Ecological Research and Development Group (ERDG), https://www.horseshoecrab.org/misc/erdg.html

Horseshoe Crab Recovery Coalition, https://hscrabrecovery.org/

Books and Field Guides

Crab Moon by Ruth Horowitz

High Tide for Horseshoe Crabs by Lisa Kahn Schnell

Crab Wars by William Sargent

I have been rescuing horseshoe crabs since I was six years old. Last year was my first season of going on every trip with my dad. Fridays in May and June, we rescued crabs on five different beaches on the Delaware Bay. Some mornings we got up at 2 a.m. so we could arrive at low tide. It's really cool to be on the beach before the sun comes up! We saved over 11,000 horseshoe crabs this season. Here are some photos from our adventures.

Horseshoe crabs trapped behind an old bulkhead

These are the crabs rescued from behind the bulkhead.

Taking a break after a long rescue day

Horseshoe crabs trapped at the base of a seawall

— CHAPTER 4 —

NIGHT LIGHTS

INVITATION TO ADVENTURE

Help keep the lights on! No, this is not a campaign to waste electricity. As the sun goes down, your backyard becomes a display of predation and promise. Fireflies light up across the continent to attract mates and, for some, to lure an unsuspecting meal close enough to devour. Our backyards, gardens, and local parks are home to various wildlife species, and many of these inhabitants are invertebrates, such as fireflies. **These small garden species play important roles in our backyard ecosystems—pollinating plants, keeping other insect populations in check, building soil, and feeding other species; however, they are being affected by pollution and loss of habitat.** It can be difficult to collect good data on many insect species, but some provide us with easier opportunities! Showy species such as butterflies can be easy to observe, and the flash of fireflies makes their presence known as well. This adventure is potentially right out your back door! Join an existing effort or start a new project in your region counting the flashes emitted during their nighttime performances.

Super macro close-up firefly. *Photo credit: khlungcenter/Shutterstock*

DID YOU KNOW ?

Fireflies use a special chemical called luciferin in the presence of oxygen to light up. This process is called bioluminescence.

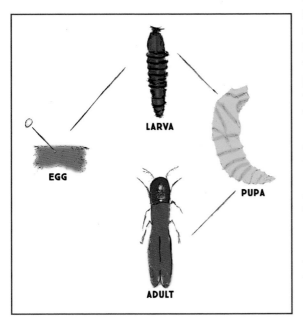

LARVA

EGG

PUPA

ADULT

Firefly life cycle

Fireflies, also called lightning bugs, are neither flies nor bugs (bugs are actually a specific group of insects). Instead, they are beetles. The most diverse group of insects, beetles are found everywhere. Cousins to the familiar ladybird beetles (also called ladybugs), fireflies can be found in some of the same habitats. Normally, insect studies require collection. Many different kinds of traps are used, set at day or night, to catch various insect species, but it is part of the biology of the firefly that allows us to study them without catching any.

Though species of fireflies can be found across the United States, there is greater diversity in the East. Their habitat is diverse—like fireflies themselves. The more than 150 species of North American firefly occupy habitats that include meadows, forest edges, and fields. Many of these habitat types can be found in your backyard or close by in a park or garden. Though they do not need to be close to large bodies of water, they do need ready access to moisture. Consuming small invertebrates as larvae (see the insect life cycle above), as adults they consume other insects (including other fireflies) and plant food such as pollen or nectar. Their diverse diet makes them important, since they control the populations of other invertebrates and pollinate various types of plants.

Though not all fireflies are bioluminescent, most species do display the almost magical flashing for which they are known. It is this part of their biology that makes them so familiar to many kids and adults and makes them useful as biological indicators. Sharing habitats with many other insect species, fireflies can serve as indicators of environmental health. In backyards, gardens, parks, and forests where firefly populations are thriving, this indicates an ecosystem that is more likely to be healthy for other creatures. However, low numbers of fireflies, or their absence in suitable habitat, can indicate just the opposite—that something is causing the habitat not to be able to support invertebrates. **Not only can you create habitat that is firefly friendly in your backyard, school garden, or local park, but you can also monitor their populations during the spring and summer.** This will allow you to determine if local habitats are healthy for fireflies and other types of invertebrates—insects, spiders, crustaceans, worms, and snails, among others!

DID YOU KNOW ?

Some adult female fireflies look like larval insects, do not have wings, and may emit a constant light from the ground. These fireflies are known as glow worms!

Backyard habitat for fireflies—tall, diverse vegetation

MONITORING FIREFLY ACTIVITY

The July storm had passed quickly and a warm, wet breeze swept across the backyard. With the sun setting, we were approaching count time. This count was my nightly adventure, a short activity that ushered in every evening during mid-May through July. Across my hometown, six families would be monitoring firefly activity. Each family's garden had their own features—flowers, trees, grasses, wood piles, and fences. We started this project to see how firefly activity would vary from one backyard to the next, and to see if we might be able to figure out why.

Our study each night was fairly simple—just after sunset, count the number of flashes we could see in our backyard during one minute. Wait 10 minutes and repeat, and then once more after another 10-minute break. We would have three one-minute counts. By adding the three counts together and then dividing by 3, we would have an average. **This number, along with our notes on temperature, wind, humidity, and precipitation amounts for the day, would be entered into our field notebook.**

Fireflies in a dark field at night. *Photo credit: Fer Gregory/Shutterstock*

Armed with my stopwatch, I stepped into the garden, took a couple of deep breaths, and waited for the start. A few flashes caught my attention, but I had to wait to count for our designated start time of 8:30 p.m. This is the time our group agreed to count our first flashes. With the sun dropping below the houses behind my backyard, it was getting close to start time. The clock ticked to half past eight, I started the stopwatch, and the count was on.

Here are the findings over a three-night period for three different backyard gardens. The random light spots represent the average count from the three different gardens. Note: these counts will be used in the activity that follows.

Flashes in the dark

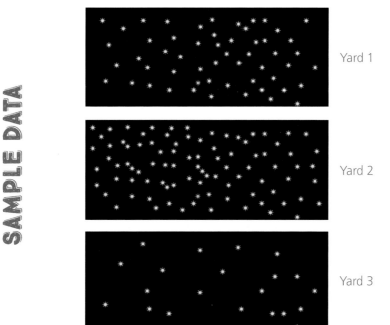

Yard 1

Yard 2

Yard 3

The three yards represented in the above diagram are all in the same town and the flashes shown were documented at the same time on the same three nights. Each garden is about the same size and the data was collected with the same methods.

FIND OUT...

- **How many flashes were documented in each of the three gardens?**
- **Identify two reasons that could explain why the flashes were different in the three gardens.**
- **Explain how your answers could result in differences in the number of flashes.**

A backyard inventory is perhaps the easiest type of community science study to conduct. You can discover something new about even some of the most common creatures by making observations in your garden. If you do not have a garden or yard, plan your surveys in a local park or at a neighbor's home. Be sure to get permission from your neighbor, check after-dark rules at your local park, and, as always, never conduct a survey by yourself.

The materials needed for a firefly study are also very simple. All you will need is a phone or stopwatch to document a minute (or other period of time, depending on your study) and a field notebook to record your counts and local conditions and site description. **Be sure to conduct your count at the same spot every night.** Ideally this will be in a location that allows you to see the greatest area of your garden or study site. You can also document your study by capturing images of your site. If you want to examine your study subject up close, bring along a small net and collecting jar to examine your fireflies. Make sure there are air holes in the top, and it is best to put some fresh vegetation in your jar for the fireflies to perch on while you are checking them out! Make sure when you are done to let them go, and if you handle them, be careful, as they are delicate.

Firefly taking flight. *Photo credit: Suzanne Tucker/Shutterstock*

Nighttime brings mosquitoes in many areas, so be sure and wear a long-sleeve T-shirt and long, light pants. A bandana will help keep insects off your neck, and a cap will do the same for your head. If you are going to use insect repellent, make sure to apply it away from your survey site, since you do not want to repel the fireflies! Consider a natural, plant-based option.

This is a great community science study to share with your younger siblings, other family members, and neighbors and friends. Get others excited about your study and you may find a new team member for your project. If you have a nature club at school or in your community, see if you can get the group involved. **Check out local nature centers or conservation groups that might be interested in your data, teaming up with you, or having you join their effort to monitor fireflies.**

Though there are recommended procedures for firefly counts, consider changing some aspect of the study after you conduct your initial count. What would happen if you count later in the evening? How does the count compare when your back porch light is on or off? Will you get the same count from every location in your garden?

CHECKLIST FOR YOUR ADVENTURE

- **Stopwatch**
- **Field notebook**
- **Pencil**
- **Insect net (optional)**
- **Holding jar (optional)**

- **Camera (or phone with a camera)**
- **Water bottle**
- **Insect repellent (as needed)**

Online Resources
The Xerces Society for Invertebrate Conversation, https://www.xerces.org/endangered-species/fireflies
Firefly Conservation & Research, https://www.firefly.org/
Mass Audubon, https://www.massaudubon.org/get-involved/community-science/firefly-watch

Books and Field Guides
Fireflies, Glow-Worms and Lightning Bugs by Lynn Frierson Faust
Silent Sparks: The Wondrous World of Fireflies by Sara Lewis

Counting fireflies is fun and easy. It is also very important to help protect species in our backyard. We have been able to see fireflies at night and then see where they go in the daytime. Our favorite night was when we saw a rainbow right before dark and then a hundred flashes as we counted. The lights reminded us of a holiday celebration!

Erin and Luka examine fireflies in live jars.

Erin holds a net used for sweeping insects.

Luka searches for fireflies in the daytime.

CHAPTER 5

FINDING FROGS

INVITATION TO ADVENTURE

Fancy frogs? Then we need you! Pack your night gear for an amphibious adventure as we wander wetlands, meander meadows, and forge forests in search of frogs and toads. One of the most threatened groups of animals, they need your help because of climate-driven changes to wetland habitats, roads that divide breeding grounds, and pesticide runoff from farms and gardens. Important data is out there to be gathered—from the backyards of your neighborhood to the deep swamps and bogs of wilderness settings—to better understand these creatures. There is only one way to find out how our amphibian friends are doing . . . **visit them in their native habitat and give them an ecological checkup!**

It is likely that frogs were part of your first experience with nature, and we need to make sure that they will be there for the next generation as well! So strap on a headlamp, pull on your knee-high boots, and put your nocturnal fears away. The frogs are calling to you, and the request is "Please Help!"

DID YOU KNOW ?

Amphibians have very permeable skin and can be affected by many types of pollutants.

Frogs and toads are amphibians, the group of mostly small, four-legged, cold-blooded vertebrates that also includes salamanders. **Different from reptiles, most amphibians lay their eggs in water and do not have scales.** Their skin is very permeable—great for getting oxygen, but bad when it comes to air and water pollution. Most amphibians undergo metamorphosis—a dramatic change in body form and function as they develop from egg to larvae to adult.

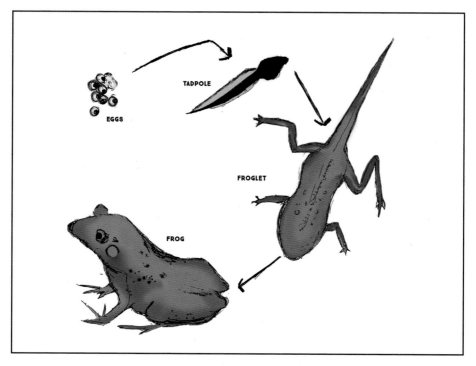

Frog life cycle

The vast majority of frogs and toads lay their eggs in aquatic habitats, and the diversity of these freshwater ecosystems that some species require can be surprising. For example, carpenter frogs in New Jersey breed in bogs and other acidic water bodies. The Pine Barrens tree frog often breeds in temporary pools, sometimes called vernal (spring) pools, which hold water for only part of the year. Breeding in these types of habitats reduces the threat from predators, since fish are usually not found in temporary pools. Some species will actually breed in watery habitats created by people. I have observed green frogs and gray treefrogs breeding in large puddles that form on sandy roads after a rainstorm!

Gray treefrog camouflaged against the bark of a tree

While they are developing within their eggs, frogs and toads get all the nutrients they need from the yolk and the movement of oxygen across the egg surface, which must be kept moist. Hatching can take anywhere from a few days to a few weeks. Emerging as tadpoles with tails and gills, they will remain completely aquatic during this stage of their life. Their diet is omnivorous (they may eat plant or animal matter) while in the tadpole stage. Developing into adults within weeks to months, they will now be able to emerge on land. As adults they will be almost exclusively carnivorous and will now breathe with lungs, though many also obtain oxygen across their skin. **Many frogs will stay fairly close to aquatic habitats, but many toads will move surprisingly far from water.**

Generally speaking, frogs are more tied to aquatic habitats throughout their lives when compared with toads. However, both breed in water, with toads typically laying a string of eggs while many frogs lay an egg cluster. Most frogs have smoother, moister skin when compared with the drier, bumpier skin of toads. There are exceptions to these comparisons, but these characteristics are helpful for identifying the basic differences.

Amphibians have life stages that require healthy habitats in both aquatic and terrestrial ecosystems. As such, they are especially vulnerable to human activities that might affect one or both of these environments. In addition, their skin is very permeable to pollutants, so pesticides and other chemicals can harm them more so than other species. Some species migrate to breeding locations, and although they may move only short distances, roads and other human features can separate needed habitat and can put them at risk from vehicles or other threats. Introduced species in aquatic habitats can outcompete frogs and toads for food, or the frogs themselves might be the food for invasive predators. **As if these threats were not enough, scientists have identified a fungus that has spread across much of the planet and is harming frog populations.** We often try to identify the cause for amphibian declines in various locations. The problem is that there are so many threats in so many areas. This is why people around the world must work together to protect frogs and toads and other amphibians!

DID YOU KNOW ?

Salamanders (another group of amphibians) need help too! In fact, North America has more salamander species than any other continent, and the United States has the greatest diversity!

A mother salamander protects her eggs—we watched them hatch!

FROG AND TOAD DATA COLLECTION

We were searching for treasure. **The Pine Barrens tree frog is the jewel of the ecosystem from which it gets its name.** Its green camouflage is complemented by a purple stripe and patches of yellowish orange. It's the type of frog you might expect to see on an expedition to the tropics of South America. But here we were searching for this species only 25 miles east of Philadelphia. Somehow almost 1 million acres of wilderness, consisting of forest and wetland habitat, has persisted here in southern New Jersey, despite being in one of the most densely populated regions of the world! Among the rare and unusual species found here is a collection of amphibians that require the healthy habitat found in the Pine Barrens.

From time to time the moon peaked out from behind the clouds, revealing the white sand trail that led us deeper into the woods. Approaching the site we had visited many times before, we stopped to review our goals. Stay in pairs. Make sure your hands are moist before handling a frog. Place them back carefully where you found them. Tick-check when finished. Just over a slight rise in the trail was a small pool where we had found various species of native frogs on past visits, and, as we stepped forward, we knew our search tonight would result in success. The characteristic "quonk" of the Pine Barrens tree frog could be heard—first a single male calling, but soon to be answered by a chorus of others.

This location, a small temporary wetland habitat (sometimes called a vernal pool), is the site we had visited each June for the past several years. On the basis of the diversity of species we find each time, we are able to establish frog community changes and how variation in temperature and precipitation can influence the presence of certain species. Even sites like this one, which is protected by thousands of acres of natural forest habitat, are sensitive to impacts such as a changing climate. Just last year, a dry spell during the spring resulted in no surface water and dramatically limited the number of species present. Other sites being monitored are closer to human features—farms, housing developments, and roads—and changes at these sites can tell us how frogs and toads are affected by both natural and human changes over time.

Pine Barrens tree frog perched in a shrub

On this night we documented every species that should be actively breeding this time of year! So for now, this habitat and amphibian community are healthy. One thing is certain—we will be back again to check on our amphibian friends!

SAMPLE DATA

The picture on the left shows some of the species documented during a June frog-and-toad survey in the Pine Barrens of southern New Jersey.

Handfuls of frogs

FIND OUT...

- Using the Online Field Guide for Reptiles and Amphibians provided by the New Jersey Division of Fish & Wildlife, identify which species are included in the photo, and provide a general description. You can access the guide at https://www.state.nj.us/dep/fgw/ensp/fieldguide_herps.htm.

What features allow you to differentiate one from the others?

Field trips to monitor amphibians require special preparations, since most surveys take place at night and near water. Not all sites may allow visitors. If you are planning a trip to a local park or preserve, be sure to check with staff to make certain that you are allowed to be there. It is likely that they will require details of your visit, including times, the group's size, and where you are planning to be during your survey. Careful planning must include a site visit in the day, so as to identify features that you may need to work around (such as fallen trees, thickets, human structures) or

that could be very helpful in recognizing a small location at night (such as a large tree, a fork in the path, a trail marker). **For your personal safety and comfort, remember that you will likely be moving around near or even in the water, so closed-toe shoes are a must.** Either boots or old sneakers will be fine. If water entry is possible or needed, again be certain to visit the site with an adult before you come back at night, and avoid locations that may have deep water or steep banks. Long pants and a long-sleeve T-shirt will best protect your legs and arms from brambles, twigs, and mosquitoes. A bandana, either tucked under a baseball cap or around your neck to keep bugs off, is highly recommended.

One of the most important considerations is the safety of the frogs and other creatures you may encounter. Remembering that these animals are very sensitive to pollutants, wearing bug spray can pose risks to the very frogs you are here to see and document. If you feel as though you must wear insect repellent, perhaps you can be the data collector; that is, the person who documents the night's diversity and habitat conditions. **You should not handle frogs or move about in their freshwater habitat if you have any chemicals on your skin or clothes.**

This brings us to the subject of ticks. Present in almost every terrestrial habitat, ticks are parasites that seek to attach to a host. Like with mosquitoes, the small amount of blood they take is used for reproduction. I always recommend that people wear long pants and a long-sleeve shirt, tuck their pants into their socks, and, perhaps most importantly, check multiple times over the next day or two for ticks on your clothing or body. All clothing worn while in the field should immediately go into the laundry, and no matter what time it is when you arrive home, you should take a thorough shower along with doing your tick check. Everyone should reference tick information provided by local, state, or national organizations. Having said all this, I will emphasize that I would not let a fear of ticks or insects keep me from an outdoor adventure. **Just be prepared!!**

Amphibian habitat in the Pine Barrens

You will find when you arrive at your site at night that the nocturnal world can look very different from what you saw in the day. Headlamps are a great investment, since they can light your way while your hands are free. Be sure to pack a water bottle, a change of clothes in case you get wetter than you planned, and snacks to keep your energy level up. Be patient and remember to stay with a partner, listen to directions provided by your group leader, and treat all creatures gently. Be sure to have an experienced group member show you the way to hold a frog.

You will want to document your adventure, so bring a camera or use your smartphone, but remember the habitat you are in and secure your devices in a waterproof case. You have come to your site to document diversity and contribute to the conservation of amphibians. If you are going to share your images or adventures, do not share geographic information with social media posts. The site you have just visited may harbor amphibians or other species that are protected, and it is often best to share the geographic details of your survey only with conservation groups or others who will use the data to protect identified species.

This may seem like a lot to consider, but remember, you are a scientist!

CHECKLIST FOR YOUR ADVENTURE

- Long Pants
- Long-sleeve T-shirt
- Bandana
- Baseball cap (or other hat)
- Headlamp (pack extra batteries)
- Closed-toe shoes
- Water bottle

- Field guide to amphibians (Peterson, National Audubon, and National Geographic, among other options)
- Extra set of clothes
- Camera (or phone with a camera)
- Waterproof case for your camera/phone

Online Resources

US Fish & Wildlife Service, https://www.fws.gov/program/endangered-species

USGS Frog and Toad Quiz, https://www.pwrc.usgs.gov/frogquiz/index.cfm?fuseaction=main.lookup

National Geographic Kids, https://kids.nationalgeographic.com/wacky-weekend/article/frogs

Books and Field Guides

National Audubon Field Guide to Reptiles and Amphibians of North America by John L. Behler and F. Wayne King

Peterson Field Guide to Reptiles and Amphibians: Eastern & Central North America by Robert Powell, Roger Conant, and Joseph T. Collins

Stokes Field Guide to Amphibians and Reptiles by Thomas F. Tyning

In Search of Lost Frogs by Robin Moore

National Geographic Readers: Frogs! by Elizabeth Carney

We spent an amazing night in the Pine Barrens searching for frogs. We saw and heard so many! My favorite was definitely the Pine Barrens tree frog, because of its beautiful color and its interesting call . . . it quonks!

Frogs seem like such common animals, but some of them are endangered species. I can't wait to return again next spring. I hope we find the same species at our site!

Sasha with a Pine Barrens tree frog

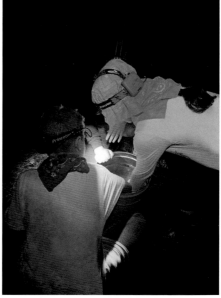

Sasha and Gabe check on the diversity of frogs temporarily held in a bucket.

— CHAPTER 6 —

MYSTERY MUSSEL

INVITATION TO ADVENTURE

In the streams and riverbeds of North America, biological riches can be found. Though you cannot keep the treasure you find, the reward is as valuable as any. These little gems are the dozens of species of freshwater mussels that may be found in the natural streams and rivers flowing through healthy landscapes, with some even being found in the urban rivers of major population centers. Join us to search for the most imperiled group of animals on the continent! **To encounter a freshwater mussel is to meet an organism that can live 100 years, one that provides important services to the river, uses amazing strategies to reproduce, and, perhaps most interestingly, tells us a story of the health of its habitat.** Team up with other intrepid invertebrate investigators and tell the story of your stream or river through the bottom-dwelling bivalves that need your help!

Photo credit: Roger L. Thomas/ Drexel University

Mussel in a streambed

Not as well known as their edible marine cousins, freshwater mussels are a diverse group of bivalve mollusks that live embedded in the sand, silt, mud, and pebble bottoms of streams and rivers around the world. They vary in size from the tiny littlewing pearly mussel to the giant Chinese pond mussel (they have cool names too!). **Regardless of size or shape, every mussel has two shells held together by a strong muscle (mussels have muscles!).** Moving along the bottom, a mussel will partially bury itself in the river bottom by using an extendable body part called the foot. Once in place, the mussel can bring in water to feed on small bits of organic matter and tiny organisms. The filtered water is then released back into the aquatic habitat. Oxygen is also obtained in this way.

Mussels reproduce by spawning—the male releases sperm into the water, which is then taken in by the female to fertilize the eggs. The resulting larvae develop into glochidia (an early life stage), which then must be released by the female and attach to the gills of a passing fish so they can be distributed to another location where habitat may support a young mussels. This is how a mussel population can move upstream against the current!

Photo credit: Roger L. Thomas/ Drexel University

DID YOU KNOW ?

Some freshwater mussels have reproductive structures that mimic small fish that other larger fish want to eat. When they approach for a bite, the developing young mussels are released to attach to the fish's gills!

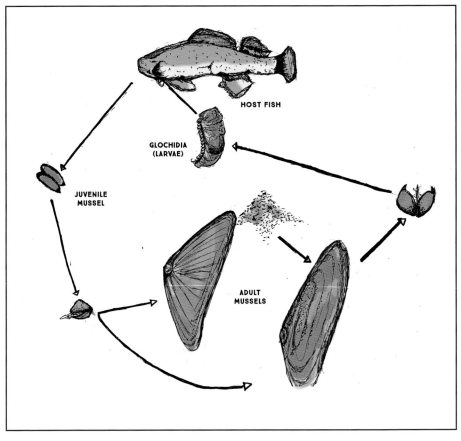

Mussel reproduction

As mussels filter the water that flows past, they help clean the stream or river of excess particles, algae, and organic matter that could otherwise increase to unhealthy levels. Mussel larvae and adults are also part of freshwater food webs, with many species of aquatic animals relying on them for food, as well as terrestrial species that visit the water searching for a meal.

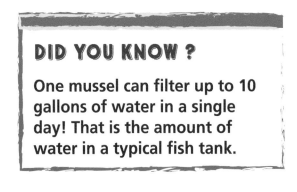

DID YOU KNOW ?

One mussel can filter up to 10 gallons of water in a single day! That is the amount of water in a typical fish tank.

Even dead mussels can be important for freshwater habitats. The shells of mussels can accumulate and create a firm surface upon which other species can live. **The diversity of habitats in a healthy stream or river is made possible by mussels!**

Perhaps the most endangered group of animals you have never heard of, they are very accessible to those who seek them out. Because they live in freshwater habitats that flow across the landscape, we can predict the health of their populations and communities on the basis of the land use around their watery homes. The land that drains into a body of water is called a watershed. As water flows across, near, and through forests, farms, cities, and streets, nutrients, sediment, and many other potential pollutants can end up in a stream or river. The filter-feeding habits of mussels can result in the accumulation of toxic chemicals in their bodies. Where sediment levels are high, their habitat—and even the mussels themselves—can be covered over. As streams and rivers are dammed and diverted, changes in water flow can change their habitat. The fish species that are needed for their successful reproduction can be affected similarly by changes in water quality and flow, and so even if mussels hang on in a habitat, without their fish partners, successful reproduction can be affected. Other threats include invasive species that may outcompete the mussels for food and habitat, and climate change, which can alter water levels or dry out shallow streams.

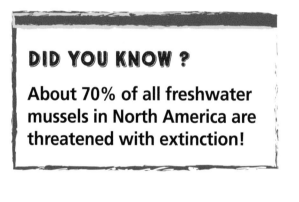

DID YOU KNOW ?

About 70% of all freshwater mussels in North America are threatened with extinction!

NOTES FROM THE FIELD

MEASURING THE MUSSELS

Less than 15 minutes from our home flows the North Branch of the Cooper River in southwestern New Jersey. Our town is found within the watershed of the same river. Driving to the site, there is very little natural landscape. Highways, parking lots, residential areas, and other urban features dominate our view. Only when we pull into a parking area next to a ball field do we see the ribbon of trees found along the banks of the Cooper. Having reviewed the Partnership for the Delaware Estuary maps, we figured mussels should be present in this stretch of the river.

Riverside habitat near our mussel study site

Only a few miles from Philadelphia, Camden County Park offers refuge to human visitors and resident wildlife alike. Walking along the footpath compacted by the feet of thousands of visitors, we find an access point to the muddy banks of the meandering river. Our team of five community scientists walks through a fragrant meadow of goldenrod and other wildflowers and arrives at the river. Placing our packs on a log, we pull on our chest waders, which will offer more than enough coverage in the knee-deep water. Scouting along the bank, we decide this site is worth searching. The bottom habitat is diverse, with sections of sand, mud, and fine gravel. Vegetation lines much of the bank, and there are a few safe areas to enter and exit the water. A couple weeks ago we visited a site nearby but decided against a survey, since a heavy rain the day before had brought water levels a bit too high to be safe, and the bottom was hidden by heavier levels of sediment. No rain in the forecast today! Ready to go with waders on, we reviewed the game plan. Two would enter the water, measure the depth and water temperature, and make their way upstream. Any sediment that enters the water column would wash downstream behind the searchers. **Aquascopes, large plastic tubes with a snorkel mask cap at the end, would allow for inspection of the stream bottom.** Another team member would follow along the bank to identify potentially good sites to search a little more carefully. The remaining two members set up the makeshift station for measuring and documenting any specimens we might find.

Gabe and Astanah with aquascopes

We were optimistic and took out the calipers, small instruments used to measure exact dimensions of a mussel's shell. Just as we were finishing the setup of our data station, our in-stream partners revealed their first find. This was promising. A large empty shell, both sides still attached, was found along the exposed portion of a sandbank next to the river. The specimen was carefully passed up. It was one of the species we were guessing would be found in this stretch of the river, the alewife floater. We measured length, width, and height and took many images on the white background of our mussel board. Even empty shells should be returned, so we passed the specimen back to the team, who returned it to where it was found.

Twenty minutes later, a second individual was found—this time a live mussel! It was the same species as before, but the shell of this one was a good bit smaller than the empty one. The habitat was described and GPS location documented as we carefully took our measurements and several pictures. Again, we placed the mussel back carefully where it was found.

Another hour of searching would turn up a broken fragment of what could have been a second species, but, without a full shell, we were not certain about the identification. As a reminder of the fact that we were not searching in a pristine habitat, *Corbicula* clams were everywhere. These bivalves were introduced into North America decades ago and have spread across the continent. Though their presence initially created some excitement, since the idea of dozens of freshwater mussels all clumped together would have indicated a healthier habitat, we left piles of the clams along the banks for the raccoons to eat.

Mussels on a whiteboard

An hour and a half later, the wader-clad pair slipped their way up the bank, and we gathered back along the log where our packs were placed. Tugging on their thick boots, our mussel searchers were freed from the heavy chest waders. We documented the finish time and checked over our data to be sure we had not missed any details of habitat, measurement, or weather. **Though only one mussel had been found, its presence was as useful an indicator as an entire bed.** Two other species should be here, on the basis of the data and maps from the Partnership for the Delaware Estuary, so we decided to return again. Celebrating the team's find for the day, we looked forward to our next mussel adventure.

SAMPLE DATA

The mussel below was found at a field site in the Delaware watershed. Notes about the site and bottom habitat are provided. The image is to scale; that is, the exact size of the specimen found.

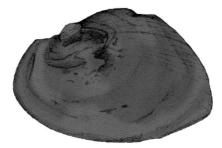

Field Notes:
Site description—small stream in a forested habitat
Water depth = 25 cm
Water temperature = 23°C
Bottom type—small rocks and pebbles with some stretches of sand

FIND OUT...

Using the online field guide from the Partnership for the Delaware Estuary, identify the freshwater mussel species shown here. Access the guide at https://delawareestuary.org/science-and-research/freshwater-mussels/.

- **Measure the mussel in inches.**
- **Identify the species of mussel using your measurements and the notes from the field site.**
- **Look up the conservation status of the species and discuss what finding this mussel tells you about the habitat and surrounding landscape from which it came.**

Searching for freshwater mussels requires both patience and persistence. Unlike birds, with their colorful feathers, or frogs, with their identifiable calls, mussels are easy to miss. Their inconspicuous presence in their aquatic habitat requires close inspection. Because they are found in water, special caution must be used when searching for them. Like any other community science study, partnering up is a must. Staying together and carefully surveying the places where you will search are important. Visits to potential survey sites are needed to identify hazards, find access to the stream or river, and decide upon safe and potentially good sites to search. Local parks and preserves are good starting points. Communicate with park officials and landowners about your interest in conducting a mussel survey, and be sure to get permission before you venture out and in! The water levels and flow of rivers and streams, especially in urban locations, can change quickly and become unsafe in a short period of time. **Check the weather before you go, and review your plan with someone who knows about the site you are looking to survey.**

The North Branch of the Cooper River—our study site

Bottom habitat may have sharp rocks, broken glass, and other debris. In fact, some freshwater mussels have sharp edges to their shells! Proper footwear is essential. Closed-toe shoes that will stay on your feet are required, and knee-high boots or hip or chest waders are best, since they will also keep you dry. Protecting your hands is important as well. Thick gloves that fit well to your hands will do the trick. Like any other field adventure, prepare for sun, heat, and insects and other creatures. Never let hasty preparations turn your adventure into an uncomfortable situation that will get in the way of your enjoyment and your success. Be sure that two people are ready and able to get into the water, and have at least one more partner on the bank, ready to support your search and efforts.

Identifying mussels can be tricky. Take care to repeat measurements, get lots of images of your specimen(s), and note location (latitude and longitude if possible) and habitat, since all these will help you identify your species. Borrow equipment from your school or a local nature center (digital thermometers are easy to use and read). Find out the local or regional groups that are involved in freshwater mussel research and conservation. Communicate with them before you plan your adventure, since they may already have sites that are in need of survey.

Perhaps most importantly, many mussel species are imperiled and are protected by law. Handle minimally and do not keep live specimens out of the water for long. Be sure to place them back exactly where and as you found them. Do not take live or dead mussels from their habitat! Report your data, since it will surely be important to the local or regional conservation efforts.

CHECKLIST FOR YOUR ADVENTURE

- Knee-high boots, hip or chest waders
- Thick gloves
- Calipers or ruler (to measure mussel specimens)
- Meter stick—to measure river/stream depth
- Thermometer—to document water temperature
- Hat
- Bandana
- Sunblock
- Insect repellent
- White waterproof board
- Camera (or phone with a camera)
- Field guide to freshwater mussels
- Backpack
- Water bottle
- Aquascope

Online Resources

National Geographic,
https://www.nationalgeographic.com/animals/article/freshwater-mussels-die-off-united-states
The Xerces Society for Invertebrate Conversation,
https://xerces.org/publications/brochures/freshwater-mussel-conservation-guide-to-saving-unsung-heroes-of-our-waters
Partnership for the Delaware Estuary,
http://delawareestuary.org/science-and-research/freshwater-mussels/

Books and Field Guides

North American Freshwater Mussels: Natural History, Ecology, and Conservation by Wendell R. Haag

Immersion: The Science and Mystery of Freshwater Mussels by Abbie Gascho Landis

Wearing waders in the river felt strange. I had never done something like this before, and it was exciting. It was cool to be able to see the bottom of the river through the aquascope. We found many interesting things in and near the river. It is sad to think that some areas of the river where many mussels were once found now have few or none. I can't wait for our next search and hope we find some live mussels.

Astanah inspects a specimen.

Gabe and Astanah hold freshwater mussels.

Astanah and Gabe on the hunt for freshwater mussels

CHAPTER 7

THE LANTERNFLIES HAVE LANDED

INVITATION TO ADVENTURE

The headlines read "Problematic, Pesky Planthoppers Present in Park and Playground!" The harmful lanternflies landed in the mid-Atlantic and began hopping and hitching their way north, south, east, and west. These colorful and interesting insects were accidentally introduced into Pennsylvania a few years ago and are on the move—sucking tree sap, releasing sticky dewdrops, and disrupting the ecology of woodlands, farms, and gardens. So many community science projects focus on species that are in trouble. This time we are called to halt the spread and limit the population of an invertebrate that has found great success in its newfound habitats.

This mission will require creativity, persistence, and the ability to round up the hordes of lanternflies that will hop their way from one state to the next unless we act quickly. Search your garden, the shade trees that line your street, the local park, and the woodland trails close to home, and let's catch some lanternflies!

Lanternfly on Virginia creeper in a local park

Native to China, India, and other countries in Asia, the spotted lanternfly is not a fly, as its name might suggest, and not a moth, as its appearance might suggest, but instead it's a leafhopper. The lanternfly belongs to a group of insects called "true bugs" or Hemiptera, meaning "half-winged," and all members of the Hemiptera have antennae that are divided into small segments and wings that are thicker at the base, with the wing overlapping at their tips. **With about 80,000 different species, the group is very diverse, but all species, such as the spotted lanternfly, have piercing or sucking mouthparts.**

Lanternflies arrived in Pennsylvania in 2012 on a shipment of landscape stone, and their first outbreak was described two years later. Lanternflies undergo incomplete metamorphosis (unlike the more familiar life cycle of the butterfly, which uses complete metamorphosis). The eggs hatch from gray, puttylike deposits on trees and other surfaces in May and June. Over the next several weeks the larvae progress through four stages called instars. The first stages reveal a small black bug with white spots, and right before developing into adults the final instar shows black and red with white spots. The adults, about an inch long, have the namesake spots, and when the wings open, flashes of red color are seen with black-and-white coloration. Males and females have yellow abdomens, but females also have red tips at the end of the abdomen. Mating occurs around August, and the laying of eggs can take place through November. Freezing temperatures will kill the adults as fall approaches winter.

In North America, lanternflies feed on ailanthus, or tree of heaven, as a preferred food source. Piercing the surface of its host plant, the lanternfly sucks the sap. Other trees for the lanternflies include black walnut, maples, tulip poplar, and black cherry. Agricultural crops affected by feeding lanternflies include grapes, peaches, apples, and hops. Damage to trees and crops can be significant, since the plants are left weaker

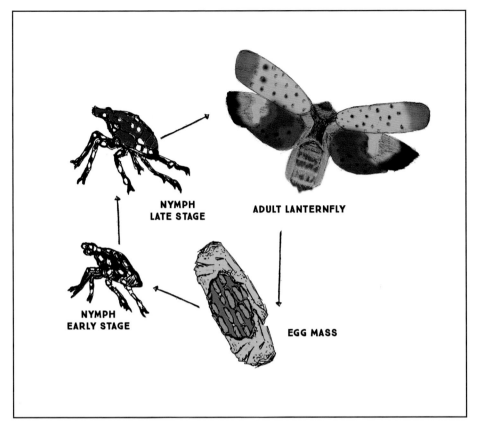

Lanternfly life cycle

and less protected from other insects and disease. The insects excrete "honeydew" as they feed, and this sugary material can result in growth of sooty molds, which makes crops unsuitable for sale.

Lanternflies are now well established in several states and have been spotted (no pun intended) in many other states. Though they are poor fliers, they can move considerable distances, and egg masses, larvae, and adults travel readily by human activity. Hitching rides on cars, trucks, trailers, and anything else that humans move around on, the lanternflies can move many miles in a surprisingly short period of time. The battle to halt their

The ailanthus tree is a favorite food source for lanternflies.

movements and reduce damage where they exist is coordinated by state agriculture agencies and county and municipal staff, and research assistance is provided by universities. Campaigns to minimize the movement of eggs and adults across state and county boundaries are underway, and various trapping methods have been used to catch larvae and adults. Residents are encouraged to scrape egg masses from trees and other surfaces, and the removal of host trees and plants can limit their population. As more is learned about lanternfly activity and movement, communities are hoping to find greater success with their control. **No doubt new methods and data will bring about even more strategies as we work to keep these invading insects in check.**

Lanternfly trap in a local park

DID YOU KNOW ?

Some insect traps can harm populations of beneficial insects and other animals. We must plan carefully when designing and placing traps on trees and other locations.

HALTING THE SPREAD OF LANTERNFLIES

On a beautiful spring morning we gathered to clean up the pollinator garden in the center of town. We raked the dry leaves and other plant debris that had insulated the ground over the winter. We bagged the leaf litter, piled up next to the garden, for composting. The air was cool, but the warmth under the vegetation brought out the sweet smell of spring soil. From the top of the brown paper bag, a small black invertebrate hopped out. It landed on our shovel handle and sat long enough for us to observe it more closely. A lanternfly larva, black with white spots, seemed to stare back at us, and only when we went to scoop the creature for closer inspection did it bounce off the shovel and onto the low branch of a young red maple tree next to the garden. **Lanternfly season had begun!**

Our summer would be busy with various projects, and only last year was a lanternfly survey added to the list. Our county was recently added to the state's hotspot map for outbreaks, and last summer we were busy with our daily walks and lanternfly collection. So much of our community science work focuses on protecting species in trouble, so when the group gathered last year we had to discuss the reality that this project would be different. The lanternflies we counted had to be removed from the trees where they were found, and squashed. Though it took some convincing, once we explained the damage that lanternflies cause in the surrounding woodlots and gardens and that their presence here was due to accidental introduction, our young community scientists understood what had to be done.

Our small group split into two teams, and each group monitored the shade trees found on a two-block tract, to document the presence of lanternflies on specific tree species and to estimate how many individuals were present on each tree. After counting, the groups proceeded to remove all the lanternflies they could reach. **A flyswatter attached to a long stick increased the reach for each removal effort.** The surveys, conducted most days, lasted several weeks until enough cold nights resulted in the absence of adults. During the winter we examined the trunks of trees known to have large gatherings of adults for egg masses, and any found were scraped off.

This year we are planning to experiment with homemade traps to see if our success can be increased with the traps in place. Along with other local communities, we are preparing for a long battle and hope to increase awareness in our community and participation in our project while reducing the number of lanternflies in our town.

DID YOU KNOW ?

An adult lanternfly will climb to the top of a tree, jump into the air, and catch the wind to aid its movement. In addition, they can move about 10 feet on a single jump!

Lanternfly nymphs in spring

Lanternfly stays afloat on a lake surface.

SAMPLE DATA

The following leaf samples came from trees observed on a lanternfly survey in Pennsylvania.

Red maple

Tulip poplar

Black walnut

Black cherry

FIND OUT...

• Match each leaf with the tree species and, using the links at the end of this chapter, determine if they are species preferred by lanternflies.

PLANNING FOR YOUR ADVENTURE

In the places where lanternflies are found, this project is an easy one to carry out. All stages of the lanternfly life cycle are easy to identify. Larvae and adults are found within the reach of even the younger members of your community science team. The efforts for lanternfly monitoring and collection require little in the way of equipment.

Our surveys typically took a half hour to conduct. We brought modified flyswatters (as described previously) and a field guide to trees so we could identify the host plants. For building traps, some simple tools and plans (see websites in the "Online Resources" section) will be needed, along with help from an adult who can lead a safe trap construction project. **It is important to emphasize that for invasive species management, the removal of individual organisms and the humane treatment of their disposal should be discussed within the group.** As with all outdoor activities, always go with a partner, contact local nature centers or agencies to coordinate your efforts if possible, keep good data records, and prepare for the weather.

Should lanternflies not be present in your community or nearby natural sites (this, of course, is a good thing), similar approaches and projects can be undertaken to address different invasive species. Be sure to spend the time needed to understand the case study, the best methods to use to control the outbreak, and necessary precautions for your group.

Modified flyswatter for reaching lanternflies

CHECKLIST FOR YOUR ADVENTURE

- Sturdy shoes
- Field notebook
- Pencil

- Flyswatter (modified to reach higher portions of the trunk and branches)
- Field guide to trees

Online Resources

US Department of Agriculture,
https://www.aphis.usda.gov/aphis/resources/pests-diseases/hungry-pests/the-threat/
spotted-lanternfly
PA Department of Agriculture,
https://www.agriculture.pa.gov/Plants_Land_Water/PlantIndustry/Entomology/spotted_
lanternfly/SpottedLanternflyAlert/Pages/default.aspx
Penn State Extension, https://extension.psu.edu/spotted-lanternfly
Cornell University College of Agriculture and Life Science,
https://nysipm.cornell.edu/environment/invasive-species-exotic-pests/
spotted-lanternfly/

Books and Field Guides

Identifying Trees of the East: An All-Season Guide to Eastern North America by
Michael D. Williams

Zoe takes notes on lanternfly count.

Our surveys revealed some interesting facts. In our neighborhood, adult lanternflies really like Virginia creeper vines and red maple trees. We removed over 75 from a single tree. They are beautiful, but because they can cause problems for our ecosystems and farms, we need to remove them. There are different ways to do this. At first it was difficult for us to squish them, but we knew that this is one of the common ways to control their population and spread. The most interesting observation we made was that lanternflies can swim! We saw one on the surface of a lake swim to the bank and fly away!

Ellie reaches for a lanternfly on a high branch.

Gabe stretches for the next lanternfly.

CHAPTER 8

THE GREAT SHOREBIRD MIGRATION

INVITATION TO ADVENTURE

Come out to welcome our feathered guests! The calendar says summer, but for shorebirds, migration has begun and various species are heading south from their northern breeding grounds in Canada. Some will settle on the gulf shore beaches, but others will travel thousands of miles farther south, reaching as far away as Tierra del Fuego, the tip of South America. Here along the mid-Atlantic coast, our beaches (like other North American beaches) are a stopover site—a place to rest, refuel, and prepare for the next leg of their journey. With major migration routes across the country, there are simply not enough scientists to monitor the beaches, lakeshores, and fields where these long-distance fliers stop. That's where we come in!

With a little bit of study and practice, you can learn to identify these birds, document which species are present near you, and estimate their abundance. During their short stay, we will describe their activity and document human use of the beaches or other habitats where birds are present. So come count the birds and count on a great time as you help describe the distribution and abundance of migratory shorebirds.

Shorebird habitat at North Brigantine Natural Area

NATURAL HISTORY

Not all birds at the shore are shorebirds, and not all shorebirds are found at the shore. This is a statement that offers an important point about monitoring shorebirds. The group of birds referred to as shorebirds includes over 200 species worldwide and about 50 species breed in North America, and they are typically highly migratory. They have long legs for their body size and have bills that are designed for picking and probing for food items, usually invertebrates. Though many species are found in coastal habitats—marshes, beaches, and mudflats—some do occur along riverbanks, along lakeshores, and in fields. With birds varying from less than 6 inches, such as the least sandpiper, to over 20 inches, such as the long-billed curlew, size can be useful in identifying similar-looking species.

Most species are described as gregarious; that is, they like the company of other shorebirds. The exception to their social nature is when they are breeding, with the male and female establishing a nest in an isolated location. Both parents are typically involved in establishing the nest, incubating eggs, and protecting the young. Most shorebird nests are established on the ground, and the camouflage of the parents, the eggs, and the chicks helps keep them protected from predators. Chicks develop quickly and are able to feed themselves soon after hatching, and often the parents leave the nesting grounds before the chicks.

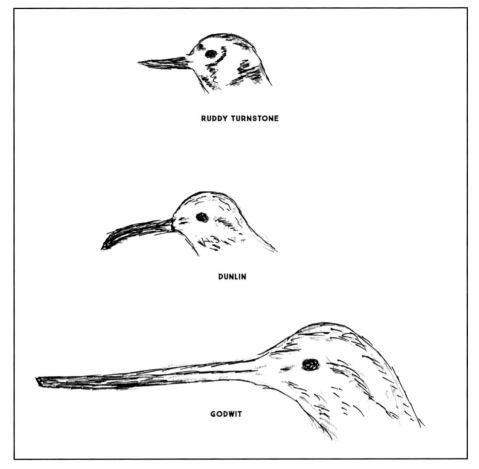

RUDDY TURNSTONE

DUNLIN

GODWIT

Three shorebird species. Note the difference in their bills.

Migration may be the most incredible part of a shorebird's life. **Some individuals can migrate thousands of miles per year and can live as long as 20 years or more.** During the longer legs of migration, a shorebird can lose about 50% of its body weight in only a matter of days or weeks. Just as amazing is that some birds can double their body weight within less than three weeks as they gorge on food to prepare for the next part of their journey. This extreme weight loss and gain is all part of a fascinating life history that depends heavily on healthy habitats with access to food.

Shorebirds require healthy habitats at their breeding grounds, wintering grounds, and often multiple stopover sites in between. Being highly migratory automatically makes a species prone to population declines. With climate changing in the Arctic tundra and coastal habitats, oil spills always being a threat along the shore, sharing habitat with humans at most stopover sites, and hunting pressure that persists in some countries, it will come as no surprise that about 75% of shorebird species are in decline and some are critically endangered. **With shorebird species widely distributed during all parts of their migration and with so many threats to their survival, the need to monitor these creatures is critical.** No matter where you live, it is likely that shorebirds can be found somewhere nearby during some season of the year. Community scientists across the globe are "adopting" locations to keep a careful eye out for an occasional visitor or predictable gatherings of tens of thousands of birds of various species. Join ranks with the scientists who, like you, care about these long-distance migrants!

NOTES FROM THE FIELD

SHOREBIRD SURVEY

The wind blowing in from the ocean was our friend on this August day. The biting flies that can chew through your clothing can be enough to clear a beach even on the most glorious of summer days. Today, with an easterly wind, they were nowhere to be found, not that we were looking for them. It was a busy day—lots of shorebirds of various species, but lots of people too! Bikers, joggers, fishers, and drivers were moving about on the beach. Vehicles moved north and south, looking for that ideal fishing spot, and walkers and joggers moved from the dunes down to the water's edge, searching for shells and the easiest ground to walk on.

With the tide being low, it was feeding time for the birds, and the flocks of sanderling, sandpipers, and plovers that gathered near the water seemed to feed frantically. Birds scurried about in the mixed flock, gobbling up amphipods, probing for small clams, and prying worms from their burrows. We paused to count a group corralled between two parked pickup trucks—50 sanderlings, 12 semipalmated sandpipers, three ruddy turnstones, and five American oystercatchers. **Using symbols to indicate species and connecting each species with the number observed, we scribbled in our field notebook.** Another pickup truck drove past, apparently coming in too close to the birds in the flock, as they flushed into the air. We started our stopwatch to determine how long they stayed in the air. The birds seemed to fly as a single organism, wheeling out over the water and then eventually settling back in close to the spot where they had been feeding.

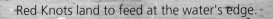

Red Knots land to feed at the water's edge.

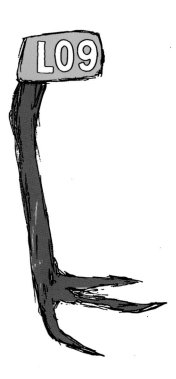

We moved farther up the beach and spotted a cluster of shorebirds and could tell by the silhouette that there was a new species in this group. Red knots! Along with piping plovers, the knots are federally listed as an endangered species (note: knots are technically in the category "threatened").

We are always glad to see this bird and are especially happy when we see juveniles mixed in with the adults. Attempting a count, we were again interrupted by a jeep that came past, and the flock moved up the beach. **We knew there were nearly a hundred, but an exact count would be much more useful to the scientists, plus we might see some birds with flags on their legs that indicated specific birds.** We followed the flock up the beach, making sure to keep back far enough so that they could continue feeding. Our time was limited. They would not be on this beach for long—southern beaches were calling.

SAMPLE DATA

Below are the average species richness (how many different species) and average species abundance (how many total shorebirds were observed) per survey for the 16-year period from 2005 through 2020 on North Brigantine Beach in New Jersey. The site is a critical stopover site for migratory birds.

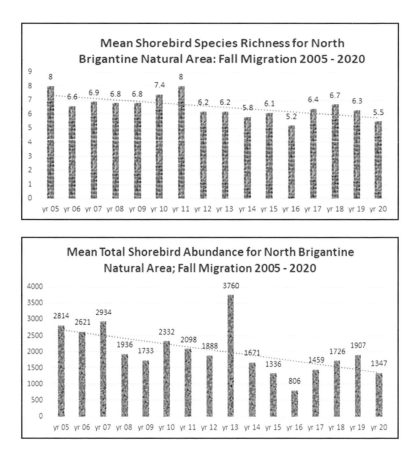

FIND OUT...

- Describe what has occurred at this stopover site for the last 16 years.
- Do richness and abundance go up and down together?
- What factors might impact richness and abundance in a given year on a beach?
- Can you think of a reason as to why the abundance was so high in 2013?

PLANNING FOR YOUR ADVENTURE

Shorebird surveys, and bird surveys in general, have gained a lot of momentum in recent years. You will likely find lots of support from local nature centers and other environmental groups. There are many resources available to birders, so take advantage of the relative ease with which you can prepare for your community science project. **Communicate with others about the goals of your study: assessing the health of the habitat, estimating the number of each species, and/or documenting the human activity at the site.** You may find that a site already has a community science effort, but that another site is in need of monitoring for birds.

Shorebird survey team

Binoculars are a must for all bird projects. Your school or local nature center may have a pair to borrow, but if you make the choice to purchase some, a visit to a local Audubon center or nature store is recommended to select the pair that is best suited for you and your project. As with all community science projects, be sure to visit your site with your family or another adult who is familiar with your project.

Certain features at your site may be helpful as you document where birds are and what they are doing at the location. It might be useful to indicate that a group of shorebirds are feeding just south of an old piling or right in front of a high dune. Though there are various efforts to establish local, regional, and global community science bird projects, eBird from the Cornell Lab of Ornithology is one of the most familiar. You can start an account through eBird that can be used for all kinds

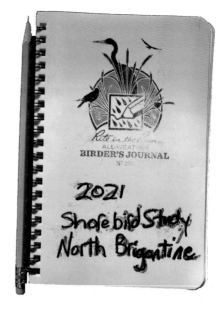

Rite in the Rain field notebook

of sightings and projects, ranging from their Project Feederwatch (https://feederwatch. org/) to long-term monitoring of an important breeding or stopover site. **Be an active learner and share your data and experiences.** Although it is important to share data through online resources such as eBird, there are many benefits to sharing your project in person, with your school and local nature center. The only thing better than a community science project and data set is sharing the experience with others!

CHECKLIST FOR YOUR ADVENTURE

- Long pants (to avoid biting insects)
- Shoes (appropriate for the habitat)
- Hat
- Backpack
- Binoculars
- Field notebook
- Pencil
- Field guide to birds
- Camera (or phone with a camera)
- Water bottle
- Sunblock (as needed)
- Insect repellent* (as needed)

Please be thoughtful about your selection of sunblock and insect repellent, since some brands have toxins that can potentially harm wildlife and humans.

Online Resources

Manomet, www.Manomet.org

Cornell Lab of Ornithology, https://www.allaboutbirds.org/news/

eBird website at Cornell, https://ebird.org/home

Books and Field Guides

Stokes Beginner's Guide to Shorebirds by Donald and Lillian Stokes

Shorebirds of North America: A Comprehensive Guide to All Species by
   Kevin Karlson

The Shorebird Guide by Michael O'Brien, Richard Crossley, and Kevin T. Karlson

Moonbird: A Year on the Wind with the Great Survivor B95 by Phillip Hoose

MORE ON SHOREBIRD SURVEY ADVENTURES
BY EMILIA (AGE 11), RONJA (AGE 11), AND NODIN (AGE 14)

There were so many birds during our recent visit! For some shorebird species there were hundreds, but for others only a few. At first we were not very good at estimating the numbers, but like everything, the more practice you get, the better you become! We saw gulls and eagles and other species as well. After 6 miles on the beach, we were tired, but we still had enough energy to collect plastic from the beach, which helps the shorebirds and all species.

Nodin takes a close look with the spotting scope.

Emilia and Ronja counting shorebirds

Emilia and Ronja take a rest at the "No Vehicles" sign.

CHAPTER 9

SOS—SAVE OUR SPIDERS

INVITATION TO ADVENTURE

What has eight legs; scrambles about in old barns, wood piles, and meadow edges; is fun to watch, though sometimes scary; and can easily hide? Four kids in search of spiders! One of the most important invertebrate groups is too often feared and seldom appreciated. **Spiders are amazing, but if you don't slow down enough to watch them, you will miss out on a curious and hardworking group of creatures.** Do a search for spiders on the internet, and most of the websites that come up will describe ways to get rid of them. Why would you want to get rid of anything that eats mosquitoes, flies, aphids, and other pesky bugs? The time has come to search for, study, share sightings, and, most of all, protect these eight-legged predators!

Join us on the newest of our community science adventures—documenting the diversity of spiders in our backyards, sheds, meadows, and woodlands. We can protect only those creatures that we know are there. From the pages that follow, a new project is born. Together we will start a spider conservation movement: SOS—Save Our Spiders!

NATURAL HISTORY

Spiders belong to the largest group of animals on Earth—the arthropods. Arthropod means "jointed foot," and all members of this group have tough exoskeletons, lack a backbone, and fill almost every possible habitat on the planet. Spiders are different from insects and other legged invertebrates, and they belong to the group known as arachnids, which they share with ticks, mites, and scorpions.

A flower crab spider waits for prey.

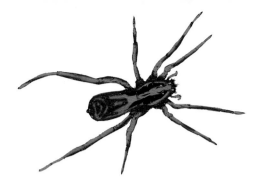

More specifically, the roughly 45,000 species of spiders belong to a subgroup all their own (called an order) known as Araneae. With a body divided into two main sections, the cephalothorax in the front and the abdomen in the back, spiders lack antennae, but all possess the ability to produce silk. The use of silk most familiar to people is the production of the web, but only about half the spiders in the world use a web to catch prey. The silk is also used by some species to make shelter, move from one location to another, and attract a mate, as well as other uses.

Just about every species of spider is a predator. Though many eat other invertebrates, some will catch small vertebrates as well, including lizards, frogs, rodents, and birds. A close-up image of a spider reveals its predatory adaptations. The chelicerae function as a spider's jaws, which are tipped with the fangs. The pedipalps are typically longer appendages that are used to sense a spider's surroundings by touch. Though they look like legs, they are not counted as such (spiders have four pairs of walking legs). **Additional information about a spider's environment is provided by the hairs that cover the body and legs. Spiders can use these specialized structures to "hear" their surroundings as vibrations.** Like the number of their walking legs, many spiders have eight eyes, though some species have fewer. Despite having multiple eyes, many spiders have poor eyesight, instead relying on touch, vibration, and taste to explore their surroundings.

DID YOU KNOW ?

Many young spiders, called spiderlings, will release a line of silk so they balloon, or kite, to a new habitat.

Orbweaver spinning its web

Fishing spider

Spiders can be found in almost every terrestrial habitat on Earth, and even some aquatic ones!

Varying greatly in body size, with some hardly visible to the naked eye while others can fill up the surface of a dinner plate, and with varying hunting strategies that allow them to catch many different species, spiders are well adapted both to natural and human habitats. Some have amazing camouflage, others can jump incredible distances, and some can spin webs within minutes. Though often unwelcomed within our homes, spiders thrive under furniture and in basements, crawl spaces, attics, barns, cabinets, and houseplants. **Both in the wild and around humans, spiders perform an important service—keeping insect and other invertebrate populations in check.** They will reduce aphid populations (which can destroy crops) and mosquitoes (which can cause disease), and they will also gobble up flies (which can ruin a picnic). Additionally, spiders are an important food source for many other species.

DID YOU KNOW ?

Some species of fishing spiders are able to stay underwater for several minutes, trapping oxygen bubbles in the hairs on their body.

Wolf spider on the hunt

In our homes, where arachnids are seldom welcomed, spiders can be harmed by pesticides and other chemicals, and often webs are destroyed as we tidy things up. The same threat persists outdoors as well, with pesticides killing prey and harming the spiders directly. As is true for many species the most harmful threat is habitat loss—clearing forest, meadows, and other natural places where spiders thrive. Additional problems arise due to climate change and the pet trade (there are a surprising number of people who like to keep spiders as pets). **Of the thousands of spider species around the world, only a very small number are being studied in enough detail to understand threats and the status of their population.** This is where you and I can help. Not only can we conduct surveys to find out what species inhabit our gardens, parks, and other habitats, but we can also spread the word about the importance of spiders and how very fascinating they are!

NOTES FROM THE FIELD

SPIDER STUDY

We knelt down on the edge of the meadow. Handed a small jar filled not quite halfway with water, I inserted the jar in the hole I had just dug in the ground. I carefully pushed soil up to the rim of the jar with one hand while covering the opening to prevent soil from dropping into the water at the bottom. The pitfall trap was now right at ground level. We set 10 traps, each a meter from the next along the edge of the meadow, and then another line (scientists call these sampling lines "transects") in the meadow interior.

Collected pitfall traps

Repeating the process at another site, we now had set 40 traps. The traps would be left overnight, since many spiders are active when the sun goes down. At another site in the same park, we used our sweep nets to sample the vegetation. The net was filled with all types of invertebrates. Though we were not able to identify every species, we did document the identity of some and then described each of the other individuals on the basis of the characteristics—small yellow spider, spider with stripes on its abdomen, tiny black spider with really long legs. Our list filled with diverse species—we counted number and richness (how many different species).

Meadow habitat

With a goal to document as many species as we could and compare this site with another site that had different plant types, we came to find that 30% of all invertebrate species found on this day were spiders! Some were found to be abundant at both sites, and others were very specific to only one type of plant at one location. We were beginning to piece together the details of spider diversity. Our homework assignments were many: find out the species names of as many as we could, describe the feeding habits of these species, compare the relative abundance of the types we found, and compare the results of the pitfall traps that were used to sample at ground level with that of the sweep nets we used to sample the vegetation. Though we wound up with more questions than answers, we knew this was the start of an important new community science project. Others will be invited to join, and our data will eventually shed light on the spider diversity and habitat here in this suburban park.

SAMPLE DATA

On a recent spider safari to a park meadow in New Jersey, one species seemed to show up in every sample. The goldenrod crab spider is a beautiful invertebrate that we would like to know more about.

FIND OUT...

• Create a species profile for the goldenrod crab spider:
  Look up the goldenrod crab spider. Describe every aspect of its natural history—body, distribution, habitat, diet, and reproduction.

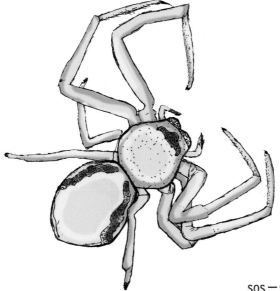

Spiders need more love from people. This will likely become obvious to you as you attempt to recruit partners for your spider project. It is tough to convince people that the small and creepy are worth saving, and perhaps even harder when that invertebrate is a spider. We are taught from a small age that spiders are to be feared, so prepare to be challenged when it comes to assembling your spider team. **Once you begin and you get a close look at a jumping spider or a crab spider or a beautiful orbweaver . . . you will be hooked!**

Spider searching will bring you into habitats and human structures that will require long pants and closed-toe shoes. Please be careful searching barns, sheds, etc. if you are seeking out spiders that live in human structures. Poorly lit older structures can have exposed nails, old boards, and rusty metal. Wear gloves and be sure to get an adult's permission before you explore areas that may have special safety concerns.

If you are preparing pitfall traps, make sure you set the jars in the ground carefully, and when you collect the jars, pick them up from the outside. Do not put your fingers down into the jar! When sweep-netting, roll the bag of the net from the outside and look in before collecting any invertebrates. **Keep in mind, you can document spiders without collecting! Best not to pick anything up with your bare hand, both for the safety of the creatures and to avoid a pinch, sting, or bite.** Gloves are a good idea! Small cardboard cups are great for holding creatures for further study or photographs, and macro lenses (check out the LaMotte macro lens) or hand lenses are useful for getting a better look.

Grace with sweep net

Grace inspects the contents.

It may be that some invertebrates do not survive the night in the pitfall trap. As such, set pitfall traps only when you are conducting a study, and do not leave pitfall traps in the ground for more than one night. Fill the holes back in when you pull the traps. When your adventure is over, be sure to check for ticks (which are arachnids, but not spiders!) when you return home. Field guides or iNaturalist can be used for working through identifications. Find out if local nature centers or museums are interested in your data. There are relatively few community science spider studies, so help spread the word about what you find!

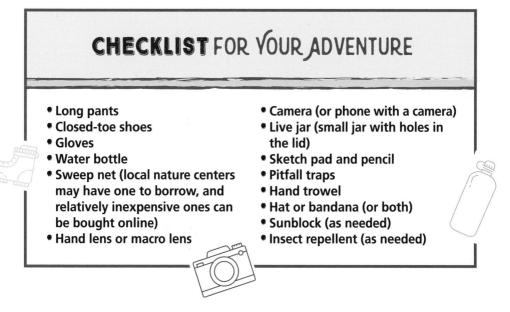

CHECKLIST FOR YOUR ADVENTURE

- Long pants
- Closed-toe shoes
- Gloves
- Water bottle
- Sweep net (local nature centers may have one to borrow, and relatively inexpensive ones can be bought online)
- Hand lens or macro lens
- Camera (or phone with a camera)
- Live jar (small jar with holes in the lid)
- Sketch pad and pencil
- Pitfall traps
- Hand trowel
- Hat or bandana (or both)
- Sunblock (as needed)
- Insect repellent (as needed)

Online Resources

Spiders Worlds, https://www.spidersworlds.com/

National Geographic,
https://www.nationalgeographic.com/animals/invertebrates/facts/spiders

Spider Conservation IUCN,
https://www.iucn.org/news/species-survival-commission/202112/
specialist-groups-allocated-fund-projects-aim-protect-lesser-
known-endangered-species

Books and Field Guides

Common Spiders of North America by Richard A. Bradley and Steve Buchanan

National Audubon Society Field Guide to Insects and Spiders: North America by
National Audubon Society

Spiders (National Geographic Kids) by Laura Marsh

MORE ON SPIDER ADVENTURES
BY OLIVER (AGE 8) AND GRACE (AGE 11)

Oliver inspects the catch.

We had a blast using the sweep nets in the meadow for catching spiders. Though we caught many types of insects as well (and they were all really cool), the spiders we caught were amazing! Some were big, others small. Even their colors were really different. The crab spiders were my favorite. They were camouflaged to blend in with the goldenrod flowers! It's amazing how many different spiders live in our area!

The promise of another sweep

Grace and Oliver—the sister/brother spider team

PART THREE

COMMUNITY SCIENCE
BEST PRACTICES

CHAPTER 10

USING YOUR FIELD NOTEBOOK AND DATA SHEET TEMPLATE

Scientists who work in the field often rely on handwritten notes to document and describe data. It is essential to capture the details of a site, the values of data collected, and the conditions that may affect the study subject.

COMMUNITY SCIENCE DATA SHEET

NOTES FROM THE FIELD

PROJECT NAME:

LOCATION:

DESCRIPTION:

TIME:

WEATHER:

PARTNER/S:

DATA/CALCULATIONS:

NOTES / SKETCHES:

Your field notebook will serve not only as a central location for your data and field notes and sketches, but also as a reference for you as you move on in your science education and reflect upon your outdoor adventures. **You may find that one of the studies you conduct will involve methods or species that could be part of another adventure later in your life.** I recommend that you include thoughts, sketches, connections, and questions in your field notebook for later discussions and explorations.

A pencil is recommended for writing in your field notebook, and color sketches are a great addition to your notes. Rite in the Rain notebooks are ideal for collecting outdoor data.

You can also use the Community Science Data Sheet template, which can be downloaded from www.schiffer-kids.com/communityscience.

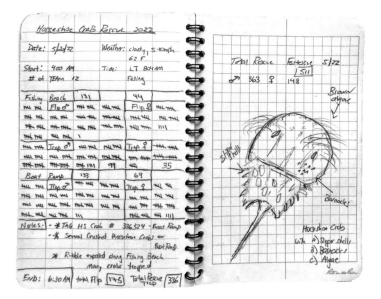

An example of data entry in a field notebook

If species identification is part of your study, there are various websites that can help, as well as field guides that can be purchased or borrowed. Several are referenced in this book. Additionally, iNaturalist offers a free app that not only can aid with identifications but can also be used to organize and share projects (https://www.inaturalist.org/).

For each study you should include the following in your field notebook:

- Title of study
- Date
- Weather conditions (temperature, cloud cover, precipitation, humidity, wind)
- Description of site
- Start and end time
- Organized and titled data tables with units

— CHAPTER 11 —

SAFETY IN THE FIELD

Staying safe while exploring outside is easy when you are prepared and organized for your adventure, communicate with your team, and always stay in a group led by a responsible adult. Most problems encountered while in the field occur when one or more of these steps are missed. Be sure to know where you are going and what problems may occur. Think about access to study sites. Is it near a busy road? Is there poison ivy? Do you have the right shoes for the terrain? **Have a plan should an unexpected storm approach.**

Biting or stinging insects occur seasonally at most sites. Wear insect repellent when needed, but also remember that some species, such as frogs, are very sensitive to chemicals that may be on your hands when you hold them or venture into aquatic habitats. Consider carefully the brands of insect repellent available. Apply appropriately and discuss with your adult leader and whole team. Recommended brands will not be toxic to you or wildlife.

Mosquito and tick bites should be addressed promptly. Access recommendations for treatment from your healthcare provider or state health agency.

The sun can make for a very pleasant exploration, but sunburn can make for a disappointing ending to a wonderful adventure. Again, consider the brand of sunscreen. Recent studies have warned that some brands are harmful to humans and wildlife alike. A wide-brimmed hat, bandana on the neck, and long-sleeve shirt will minimize the amount of skin exposed to the sun.

Dehydration is the easiest problem to avoid. Bring water in a reusable container and bring a backup! Check the forecast and temperature; consider how long you will be outside. Always bring extra water.

Bring basic first-aid supplies and consider taking a first-aid, CPR, or wilderness response course. There are opportunities to do so in most areas.

Stay safe during your community science adventures! **Staying healthy and comfortable will contribute to greater success.**

Online Resources
US Forest Service, https://www.fs.usda.gov/recreation/safety/
National Safety Council,
https://www.nsc.org/home-safety/tools-resources/seasonal-safety/outdoors
SafeHome, https://www.safehome.org/resources/outdoor-safety-health-guide/

COMMUNITY SCIENCE IN (AND OUT OF) THE CLASSROOM

It was not until my third year of college that one of my teachers took me outside to learn something about the natural world. As a child I came to the conclusion that adventures outside took place before or after school. I managed to convince my bus driver in elementary school to drop me off at any number of spots along the route home. She knew of my interest in ponds, forests, and fields and, by making it easier to access these locations, was actually one of my biggest supporters in the early days.

Wooded path in the Pine Barrens

Though I did not realize it for some time, I learned so much more than science during my adventures. Navigating woodland trails and following stream corridors, I came to understand geography and landscape. Many of the creatures I came across became the subjects of sketches and stories I would create (though my art skills never matched my interest in art). We made a point of measuring fish and calculating averages among different species that were caught in the lakes near my house. We would estimate the number of tadpoles in a small pool in the spring and then count them to see how close we came to the actual number. I suppose if someone had said we were practicing math, geography, writing, and art, we might have abandoned our activities.

Sometimes education came from unexpected places. Across the street from my childhood home lived an eccentric older lady. We called her the mushroom lady, since she could be seen carrying a basket under her arms as she wandered off into the woods looking for fungi. My brother and I would tag along, and she would teach us about edible mushrooms, rare orchids, and interesting animals. Much like some of my classroom teachers, she would give my brother and me "homework." In order to qualify for the next walk in the woods, we had to be ready to share with her our studies on the favorite food for a certain bird species or the preferred wetland habitat of an amphibian. The excitement of learning the next cool fact kept us on task, and I am sure I skipped an actual homework assignment or two from school in order to complete the mushroom works, as we came to call them.

Fast-forward many years: I decided that an environmental path was perhaps my best option after taking a few ecology classes in college. While applying to graduate school, I fell into a teaching job that I figured would be temporary. Remembering my field ecology course in college, I decided that I wanted to engage and inspire my high school students to think about science through a natural lens. Right from the start I realized that for many of them, the same spark that was lit for me was inspiring some of them to learn more as well. I stayed on for a second year and put my own future studies on hold. Two years became five, and though I eventually went back to school, it was part-time while I continued to teach (in fact, my students helped me with my research as a graduate student!). Now almost 30 years later, I continue to use what I learned from my childhood about the importance of making observations and asking questions. These are central themes in the design of my classroom, curriculum, and field experiences, all of which focus on hands-on, place- and project-based learning in community science.

As an educator I have been witness to the variation in teaching methods available to educators. **The common thread that can be found among these approaches is hands-on, explorative, inquiry-based investigations**. This allows students to practice science in a way in which every individual can use their skills, develop

Nets ready for the next adventure

DID YOU KNOW ?

You can find the guidelines for Next Generation Science Standards (NGSS) for community science adventures at www.nextgenscience.org.

partnerships, collaborate, and address meaningful questions, with emphasis on place-based study. Curiosity, creativity, and communication are to be emphasized, and practicing science by using an interdisciplinary approach while making a difference is the goal.

If you are just beginning, or as you continue, to develop community science projects, the following guidelines will help you stay on track:

- Set realistic goals.
- Reach out for collaboration and partnerships in the community and region.
- Invite your teachers and parents to participate in your project.
- Emphasize and develop the interdisciplinary elements of your project.
- Persist! Getting started can be frustrating and difficult.
- Celebrate your successes and failures.
- Share your story.

Adventure awaits! See you in the field . . .

APPENDIX

ANSWER KEY FOR "FIND OUT" ACTIVITIES

Chapter 3: Horseshoe Crab Rescue
- Total crabs rescued = 3,411
- Fortescue likely had the most human disturbance (pilings, rubble, homes, seawalls, and boat ramps), since trapped crabs are likely an indication of human structures on the beach, while flipped crabs may simply be turned over on the beach.
- Data collected at each site should include beach length, tide, weather, human features on the beach, and other wildlife.

Chapter 4: Night Lights
- Garden 1 has an average of 55 flashes. Garden 2 has 91 flashes. Garden 3 has 21 flashes.
- Differences in habitat may be the reason for the differences in data. Students may suggest water availability, vegetation cover, and the type and size of habitat patches. Pesticide use in a garden will also likely reduce firefly activity.
- Light pollution in the garden or adjacent properties may cause the differences observed in the data.

Chapter 5: Finding Frogs
- Top two frogs: Pine Barrens tree frogs; middle left: green frog; bottom left: gray tree frog; bottom right: carpenter frog. Color and pattern are the main ways to distinguish these frogs in the photograph. Description of each species as found in the online guide linked to the activity.

Chapter 6: Mystery Mussel
- Measures about 2.1 inches
- Green floater

• Endangered in New Jersey, imperiled in Pennsylvania, extinct in Delaware. Found in a stream bottom that has healthy habitat (mixed substrate/bottom material). Forested habitat along stream corridor reduces erosion and runoff of pollution.

Chapter 7: The Lanternflies Have Landed
• Top left: tulip poplar; bottom left: red maple; top right: black cherry; and bottom right: black walnut. All have been documented to be used by lanternflies. The use may be for food, cover, and egg laying and may vary by lanternfly life stage.

Chapter 8: The Great Shorebird Migration
• Species abundance shows a trend of decline for the 16-year period, though an unusual spike in abundance is observed in 2013. Species richness shows a trend of decline during the 16-year period.
• Though the abundance and richness do not show an obvious increase or decrease in the same year, it is notable that the years 2005 and 2011 have the highest richness, and the average abundance during these two years is above average for the 16-year period (over 2,000 birds per survey).
• Sometimes food availability is really good in one location or really bad in others, such that your site becomes a favorite for shorebirds. Sometimes one species may be very abundant, and large numbers can stay at one stopover spot for a prolonged period. In 2013 about 5,000 dunlins stayed at North Brigantine for a few weeks. As such, our average count for the season went way up.

Chapter 9: SOS—Save Our Spiders
• Species profile: goldenrod crab spider (*Misumena vatia*):
  Description: Adult size, 3–9 mm (0.11–0.35 inches); males often smaller than females and often have dark front legs. Colors vary from yellow to cream to white, with some red, and individuals can change color to blend with their background.
  Distribution: Found throughout North America in habitat that supports populations
  Habitat: Found in prairies, grasslands, meadows, and gardens with goldenrod, milkweed, and other wildflowers.
  Feeding: An ambush predator, the goldenrod crab spider will grab another insect or invertebrate that comes in close to where they are found. The long front legs (crab-like; hence the name) allow it to grab prey larger than itself.
  Reproduction: After mating, the female deposits an egg sac among the vegetation and will guard the eggs until the spiderlings hatch in a few weeks' time. She dies shortly after her young hatch out and disperse.

GLOSSARY

amphibian: Any species of the group of scaleless, cold-blooded vertebrates that occupy aquatic or terrestrial habitats (or both). Many start life as aquatic larvae, and almost all go through metamorphosis.

aquatic: Referring to organisms living in bodies of water

arachnid: Any terrestrial invertebrate, with most having eight jointed legs, including spiders, ticks, mites, scorpions, and others. A few species are adapted to aquatic habitats.

arthropod: An invertebrate animal with a segmented body, a tough exoskeleton, and jointed legs. The group includes insects, crustaceans, and arachnids.

biodiversity: The variety of different species living on Earth or in a specific ecosystem or habitat

biological indicator: Any species that serves as an indicator of the health of the environment

bioluminescence: The production and emission of light from an organism

biosphere reserve: An aquatic or terrestrial location designated for protecting species and habitats while allowing for sustainable use of resources

bivalve: An aquatic mollusk with a body found within a hinged pair of shells. The group includes oysters, clams, and mussels.

breeding: The processes that result in the production of offspring in animals and plants

camouflage: An adaptation that an animal uses to blend in with its surroundings

carapace: The hard external covering of arthropods. Also, the upper portion of the shell of a turtle.

carnivore: An animal that feeds on the flesh of another animal

cephalothorax: The fused head and thorax of arachnids and a few other related groups

chelicerae: Paired appendages near the mouth of certain arthropods, such as arachnids, that are modified for feeding

climate change: Long-term changes in temperature and precipitation that have resulted in an increase in the average global temperature on Earth and extreme weather events

cold blooded: Also known as ectotherms, an animal whose body temperature varies with the environment

community science: Scientific work, study or data collection (or a combination of these) conducted by members of the public to be used by the scientific community

conservation: Methods and strategies used for the planning of careful and sustainable use of natural resources such as water, forests, and wildlife

ecosystem: A biological community of organisms and their physical environment

ecosystem service: The beneficial processes provided by living organisms and ecosystems that make life possible for humans and all species

endangered species: An organism threatened with extinction. Officially, a species listed under the Endangered Species Act of 1973.

exoskeleton: A hard, protective outer covering that protects certain animals such as arthropods and other invertebrate groups

extinction: The loss or disappearance of a species or population from an ecosystem where it previously was found. Can occur from natural factors, though human-induced extinction events are emphasized in modern times.

glochidia: A microscopic larval stage of freshwater mussels

habitat: In an ecosystem, the place where a species is typically found, where resources and the physical environment are well suited to its survival

Hemiptera: Commonly called true bugs, references insects with specific mouthparts designed for sucking

herbivore: An animal that consumes mainly plant material for its nutritional needs

hibernaculum: A place where an animal undergoing hibernation takes shelter during the period of reduced biological activity.

hibernation: State of reduced activity that certain animal species undergo in order to survive periods of stress. Typical biological features include reduced activity, body temperature, heart rate, and breathing.

host plants: Plants that other organisms live on or off

hypothesis: A proposed explanation for an observed phenomenon, on the basis of limited observations and data; an educated guess

imperiled: A species whose populations have decreased, such that it is threatened with extinction. May or may not be officially listed as such.

invasive species: Any species not native to a particular ecosystem in which it is found and that causes ecological harm to the system

invertebrate: Any animal species lacking a backbone, comprising most species of animals including arthropods, mollusks, echinoderms, and various other groups

larva: The active immature form of an insect, or other animal, which often differs greatly in appearance and function

metamorphosis: Biological process in which an animal undergoes physical changes as it transitions from one life stage into another, such as larvae to adult

migration: The movement of animals from one location to another, often relatively long distance, which frequently occurs with seasonal change—to access food or habitat and/or for reproduction

naturalist: One who studies nature or natural history

omnivore: An animal that eats both plant and animal material

parasite: An animal or plant that lives in or on another organism in order to gain food or protection

pesticide: A chemical or biological agent that deters or kills an organism deemed a pest

Pine Barrens: A geographical region in New Jersey, in which sandy, acidic soil shapes an ecosystem of forests and wetlands dominated by pine trees in upland habitats

pitfall trap: A simple collection device, buried at ground level, designed to catch small ground-dwelling organisms

pollination: The transfer of pollen from the male part of a plant to the female part of the plant, carried out by insects and other animals or by wind

pollution: Any substance in the environment that is present at a level that can be harmful to living things

population: All the individuals of the same species that live in a defined geographical region or ecosystem

scientific method: An approach to studying science and establishing experimentation in order to address questions or hypotheses

spawning: A reproductive effort in which eggs and sperm are released into the environment, usually in aquatic habitats

spiderling: A newly hatched spider

steward: One who dedicates effort to protecting the environment

stopover site: A location along a migration route that is important for food or rest for a species

survey: A specific effort to collect data or information about a location, species, or phenomenon

terrestrial: Describing land-based organisms, ecosystems, or activities

threatened species: A species whose population has declined so as to be at risk for becoming endangered

toxic: Describing a chemical that causes adverse effects on an organism

transect: A sampling effort in which data is collected along a line

vernal pool: Also known as an intermittent pool, seasonal bodies of usually shallow water that offer habitat to species, often during breeding season or migration

warm blooded: Also known as endotherms, an animal whose body temperature is kept relatively stable, despite external conditions, due to its biological activity

watershed: Also called a drainage basin, the land area or surface that drains, by elevation, into a common body of water

wetland: An ecosystem in which water is found at or near the surface. Water influences soil and vegetation that grows in these areas.

wilderness: An area of land or sea (usually large) in which human activity and impact are minimal, so as to offer good-quality habitat to species found within